Editor
Erica N. Russikoff, M.A.

Editor in Chief
Karen J. Goldfluss, M.S. Ed.

Cover Artist
Tony Carrillo

Imaging
James Edward Grace
Craig Gunnell

Publisher
Mary D. Smith, M.S. Ed.

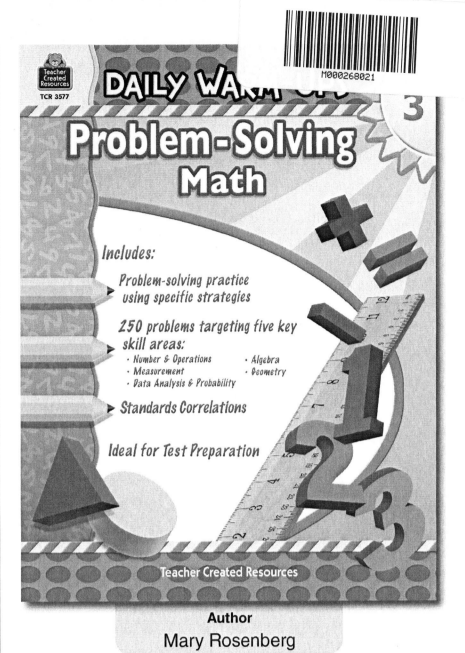

TCR 3577

DAILY WARM-UPS
Problem-Solving
Math
3

Includes:

▸ *Problem-solving practice using specific strategies*

▸ *250 problems targeting five key skill areas:*
- *Number & Operations*
- *Measurement*
- *Data Analysis & Probability*
- *Algebra*
- *Geometry*

▸ *Standards Correlations*

Ideal for Test Preparation

Teacher Created Resources

Author
Mary Rosenberg

Teacher Created Resources
12621 Western Avenue
Garden Grove, CA 92841
www.teachercreated.com
ISBN: 978-1-4206-3577-5

©2011 Teacher Created Resources
Reprinted, 2019
Made in U.S.A.

Teacher Created Resources

Table of Contents

Introduction

Problem solving develops not only students' math skills but also their logical-thinking and abstract-thinking skills. Students need to be able to recognize the important elements in a problem, identify key words that tell which math operation(s) should be used, and know which problem-solving strategy is the best choice to answer the question. The student must also compare the answer(s) to the information presented in the problem. Does the answer make sense? Does it answer all parts of the question?

About this Book

The variety of math problems in *Daily Warm-Ups: Problem-Solving Math* will provide students with enough problem-solving practice to introduce your math period every day for an entire school year. For each warm-up, allow 10 to 15 minutes for reading, interpreting, and solving the problems. Students can work on the problems in this book independently, in groups, or as a whole class. Decide which approach works best for your students, based on their math skill levels and reading competence.

The book is divided into two sections. The first section of the book introduces five specific problem-solving strategies with math problems that are not directly addressed to a specific operation or concept. The math strategies are as follows: Drawing a Diagram, Creating a Table, Acting It Out or Using Concrete Materials, Guessing and Checking, and Looking for a Pattern. (See pages 8–12 for examples of math problems to which these types of strategies apply.) The second section of the book contains more traditional problems in operations, numeration, geometry, measurement, data analysis, probability, and algebra. The general math area and focus addressed in each warm-up is noted at the top of each page.

These activities can be used in a variety of ways, but they were designed to be introductory warm-ups for each math period. The 250 warm-ups are individually numbered and should be used in any order according to your main math lessons. Choose warm-ups that cover concepts previously taught so that the warm-up can serve as a review.

Some of the questions call for counters or manipulatives. These can be used to better understand math concepts. Plastic discs, cubes, and dry beans are examples of counters and manipulatives.

Standards

The math problems in this book have been correlated to the National Council of Teachers of Mathematics (NCTM) standards and the Common Core State Standards. See the correlation chart on pages 5–7. You will find the NCTM standards and expectations along with the warm-up numbers to which they relate. As the NCTM math standards make clear, problem solving is a critical component in math instruction. It is the component that makes general operations knowledge both essential and useful. Problem solving is the basic element in the concept of math as a method of communication.

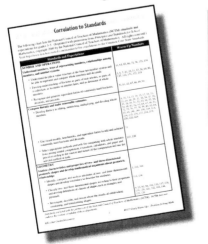

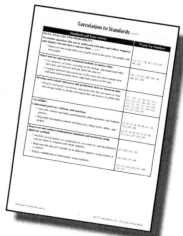

Daily Warm-Ups, Section 1

The 50 warm-ups in this section follow one of five key problem-solving strategies. Each of these pages is set up the same way, allowing students to quickly become familiar with the expectations of the problems. The answers to the problems in this section have been provided along with explanations of the thinking process behind solving each one. (See pages 163–170 for Section 1's answers.)

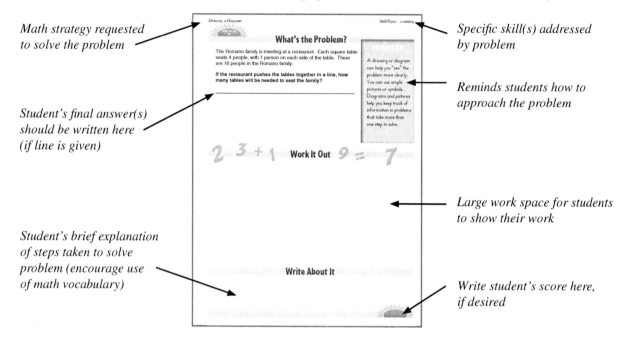

Math strategy requested to solve the problem

Student's final answer(s) should be written here (if line is given)

Student's brief explanation of steps taken to solve problem (encourage use of math vocabulary)

Specific skill(s) addressed by problem

Reminds students how to approach the problem

Large work space for students to show their work

Write student's score here, if desired

Daily Warm-Ups, Section 2

The 200 warm-ups in this section are divided into five math areas: Number and Operations, Geometry, Measurement, Data Analysis and Probability, and Algebra. Each of these pages has two warm-ups on the page. The two warm-ups relate to each other in some way. Warm-ups may be separated and given to students independently. Encourage students to apply math strategies as they solve the problems in this section.

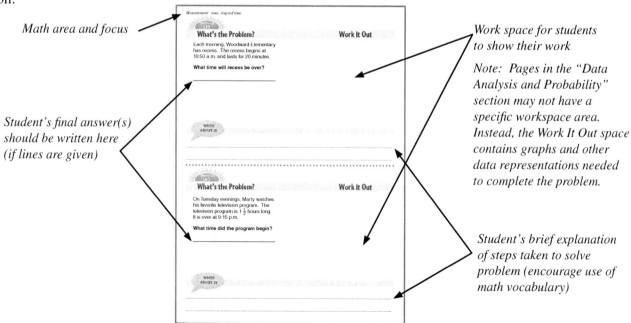

Math area and focus

Student's final answer(s) should be written here (if lines are given)

Work space for students to show their work

Note: Pages in the "Data Analysis and Probability" section may not have a specific workspace area. Instead, the Work It Out space contains graphs and other data representations needed to complete the problem.

Student's brief explanation of steps taken to solve problem (encourage use of math vocabulary)

Correlation to Standards

The following chart lists the National Council of Teachers of Mathematics (NCTM) standards and expectations for grades 3–5. (Reprinted with permission from *Principles and Standards for School Mathematics*, copyright 2000 by the National Council of Teachers of Mathematics. All rights reserved.) Visit *http://www.teachercreated.com/standards/* for correlations to the Common Core State Standards.

Standards and Expectations	Warm-Up Numbers
NUMBER AND OPERATIONS	
Understand numbers, ways of representing numbers, relationships among numbers, and number systems	
• Understand the place-value structure of the base-ten number system and be able to represent and compare whole numbers and decimals	16, 43, 65, 66, 73, 74, 173, 174
• Develop understanding of fractions as parts of unit wholes, as parts of a collection, as locations on number lines, and as divisions of whole numbers	3, 6, 7, 20, 23, 51, 57, 58, 69, 90, 137, 163, 171, 172, 219
• Recognize and generate equivalent forms of commonly used fractions, decimals, and percents	70, 81, 82, 87, 88, 89, 90
Compute fluently and make reasonable estimates	
• Develop fluency in adding, subtracting, multiplying, and dividing whole numbers	8, 10, 12, 13, 14, 15, 17, 18, 21, 22, 24, 28, 29, 31, 33, 34, 35, 36, 37, 38, 39, 51, 52, 53, 54, 55, 56, 59, 60, 61, 62, 63, 64, 67, 68, 71, 72, 75, 76, 77, 78, 79, 80, 83, 84, 85, 86, 148, 149, 150, 154, 213, 214, 215, 216, 217, 218, 219, 220, 222, 224
• Use visual models, benchmarks, and equivalent forms to add and subtract commonly used fractions and decimals	11
• Select appropriate methods and tools for computing with whole numbers from among mental computation, estimation, calculators, and paper and pencil according to the context and nature of the computation and use the selected method or tools	237, 238
GEOMETRY	
Analyze characteristics and properties of two- and three-dimensional geometric shapes and develop mathematical arguments about geometric relationships	
• Identify, compare, and analyze attributes of two- and three-dimensional shapes and develop vocabulary to describe the attributes	1, 105, 106
• Classify two- and three-dimensional shapes according to their properties and develop definitions of classes of shapes such as triangles and pyramids	113, 114
• Investigate, describe, and reason about the results of subdividing, combining, and transforming shapes	9, 25, 93, 94, 109, 110, 117, 118, 119, 120, 121, 122, 123, 124, 125, 126

Standards are listed with the permission of the National Council of Teachers of Mathematics (NCTM). NCTM does not endorse the content or validity of these alignments.

Standards and Expectations	Warm-Up Numbers
GEOMETRY	
Specify locations and describe spatial relationships using coordinate geometry and other representational systems	
• Describe location and movement using common language and geometric vocabulary	115, 116, 223
• Make and use coordinate systems to specify locations and to describe paths	91, 92
Apply transformations and use symmetry to analyze mathematical situations	
• Predict and describe the results of sliding, flipping, and turning two-dimensional shapes	107, 108
• Identify and describe line and rotational symmetry in two- and three-dimensional shapes and designs	103, 104
Use visualization, spatial reasoning, and geometric modeling to solve problems	
• Identify and draw a two-dimensional representation of a three-dimensional object	129, 130
MEASUREMENT	
Understand measurable attributes of objects and the units, systems, and processes of measurement	
• Understand such attributes as length, area, weight, volume, and size of angle and select the appropriate type of unit for measuring each attribute	2, 4, 30, 32, 40, 95, 96, 99, 100, 127, 128, 131, 132, 136, 139, 140, 153, 155, 156, 157, 158, 161, 162
• Understand the need for measuring with standard units and become familiar with standard units in the customary and metric systems	97, 98
• Carry out simple unit conversions, such as from centimeters to meters, within a system of measurement	26, 133, 134, 135, 141, 142, 143, 144, 145, 146, 147, 151, 152, 159, 160, 164, 165, 166
• Understand that measurements are approximations and how differences in units affect precision	27
Apply appropriate techniques, tools, and formulas to determine measurements	
• Select and apply appropriate standard units and tools to measure length, area, volume, weight, time, temperature, and the size of angles	5, 19
• Develop, understand, and use formulas to find the area of rectangles and related triangles and parallelograms	169, 170
• Develop strategies to determine the surface areas and volumes of rectangular solids	101, 102, 167, 168
DATA ANALYSIS AND PROBABILITY	
Formulate questions that can be addressed with data and collect, organize, and display relevant data to answer them	
• Design investigations to address a question and consider how data-collection methods affect the nature of the data set	171

Standards and Expectations	Warm-Up Numbers
DATA ANALYSIS AND PROBABILITY **Formulate questions that can be addressed with data and collect, organize, and display relevant data to answer them** *(cont.)*	
• Represent data using tables and graphs such as line plots, bar graphs, and line graphs	172, 175, 176, 187, 193, 194, 201, 202
Select and use appropriate statistical methods to analyze data	
• Use measures of center, focusing on the median, and understand what each does and does not indicate about the data set • Compare different representations of the same data and evaluate how well each representation shows important aspects of the data	138, 175, 187, 188, 194, 196 206, 207, 208
Develop and evaluate inferences and predictions that are based on data	
• Propose and justify conclusions and predictions that are based on data and design studies to further investigate the conclusions or predictions	177, 178, 179, 180, 181, 182, 183, 184, 185, 186, 189, 190, 191, 192, 195, 197, 198, 199, 200, 203, 204, 205, 209, 210, 221, 225, 226, 230
ALGEBRA **Understand patterns, relations, and functions**	
• Describe, extend, and make generalizations about geometric and numeric patterns	41, 42, 45, 46, 48, 49, 50, 111, 112, 245, 246
• Represent and analyze patterns and functions, using words, tables, and graphs	19, 41, 42, 44, 45, 47, 49, 50, 211, 212, 229, 233, 234
Represent and analyze mathematical situations and structures using algebraic symbols	
• Identify such properties as commutativity, associativity, and distributivity and use them to compute with whole numbers	227, 228, 231, 232
• Represent the idea of a variable as an unknown quantity using a letter or a symbol	235, 236, 239, 240
• Express mathematical relationships using equations	241, 242, 243, 244, 247, 248, 249, 250

Examples of Strategies

Drawing a Diagram

Drawing a diagram or picture can help you "see" a problem more clearly. Diagrams and pictures help you keep track of information in problems that take more than one step to solve. When drawing one, make sure all elements of the problem are included.

Example 1

What's the Problem?

Mr. Kutzner is building a 20-foot fence around his backyard. He needs to add a fence post every 5 feet.

How many fence posts are needed?

_____

Work It Out

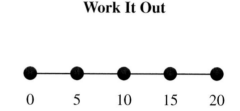

Write About It

To solve the problem, a student might draw a diagram where a line represents the 20-foot fence and each dot represents a fence post. The student would then answer the question by counting the number of fence posts.

Drawing a diagram or picture can show how an item has been shared.

Example 2

What's the Problem?

Eric has 60 marbles. He shares half with his brother, Len. Len gives $\frac{1}{3}$ of his marbles to a friend and keeps the rest.

How many marbles does each boy have?

_____

_____

Work It Out

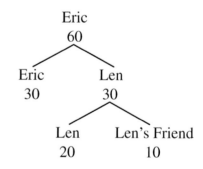

Write About It

To solve the problem, a student might draw a diagram of the marble disbursement between Eric, Len, and Len's friend. The student would then answer the question by recording the total amount of marbles for each person.

Creating a Table

Creating a table helps you organize and keep track of information. A table makes it easy to see the relationships and patterns among sets of numbers. When making a table, decide which information needs to be shown, how many columns and rows are needed, and what the headings (titles) should be. Remember to work in order and list all combinations.

Example 1

What's the Problem?

Using nickels, dimes, and quarters, how many different ways can Rosa make 75 cents?

Work It Out

# of Ways	# of Nickels	# of Dimes	# of Quarters
1	0	0	3
2	1	2	2
3	3	1	2
4	5	0	2
5	1	7	0
6	3	6	0
7	5	5	0
8	7	4	0
9	9	3	0
10	11	2	0
11	13	1	0
12	15	0	0

Write About It

To solve the problem, a student might create a table showing the different coin combinations that amount to 75 cents. The student would then answer the question by recording the number of coin combinations (ways).

Creating a table can show comparisons between pieces of information.

Example 2

What's the Problem?

Murray saves $1.00 a day and Cicely saves $9.00 a day.

How much money will Murray have saved when Cicely has saved $27.00?

Work It Out

Day Number	Money Saved— Murray	Money Saved— Cicely
1	$1.00	$9.00
2	$2.00	$18.00
3	$3.00	$27.00

Write About It

To solve the problem, a student might create a table, filling in the information until the point where Cicely has saved $27.00. The student would then answer the question by comparing Cicely's amount saved with Murray's amount saved.

Acting It Out or Using Concrete Materials

Acting it out or using concrete materials is helpful when it is difficult to visualize the problem or hard to figure out the procedure. Use real objects to create a model or use people to act out the problem and its solution. By acting it out or using objects to represent parts of the problem, you can "see" its solution better.

Example 1

What's the Problem?

Work It Out

John's foot is 5 large paper clips long.

Is your foot longer or shorter than John's foot?

_____

Write About It

To solve the problem, a student might use paper clips to measure his or her foot. The student would then answer the question after totaling the number of paper clips and comparing the total to John's length.

Using concrete materials can be helpful when comparing quantities.

Example 2

What's the Problem?

Work It Out

Alissa needs to solve this math problem.

Which is more: $\frac{1}{3}$ of 24 or $\frac{1}{2}$ of 20?

_____

Write About It

To solve the problem, a student might use cubes or other manipulatives. The student would lay out the rows of cubes into two sets, divide them according to the given fractions, and compare the quantities.

Examples of Strategies (cont.)

Guessing and Checking

Guessing and checking helps you develop reasonable guesses to solve a problem. For each guess, look at the important information presented in the problem. Check each guess against the information. Base the next guess on the previous result. Use a table to help organize your guesses.

Example 1

What's the Problem?

Evan has more cows than hens. There are four times as many cow legs as hen legs. There are 50 legs in all.

How many cows and hens does Evan have?

_____

Work It Out

Guess Number	1	2	3
Hens (2 legs)	2 hens (4 legs)	4 hens (8 legs)	5 hens (10 legs)
Cows (4 legs)	4 cows (16 legs)	8 cows (32 legs)	10 cows (40 legs)
Total Legs	20	40	50

Write About It

To solve the problem, a student might create a table to show the varied numbers of hens and cows. The student would continue to guess and check until reaching 50 legs, which is the total number of legs (provided in the question).

Guessing and checking can be used when the answer is provided.

Example 2

What's the Problem?

Paula and Robbie have 12 board games. Paula has two more board games than Robbie.

How many board games does each one have?

_____

Work It Out

Guess Number	1	2
Robbie's Board Games	4	5
Paula's Board Games	6	7
Total Number of Board Games	10	12

Write About It

To solve the problem, a student might create a table to compare the number of board games for each person. The student would continue to guess and check until reaching 12, which is the total number of board games (provided in the question).

Looking for a Pattern

Looking for a pattern is useful when the information is ordered in some way. It makes it easier to predict what comes next. Study any number pattern to see how the numbers change from one number to the next. Are the numbers increasing or decreasing? At what rate are the numbers changing? The numbers can change by adding, subtracting, multiplying, or dividing by a given number. In some patterns, two of these operations might be used.

Example 1

What's the Problem?

Max wrote this set of numbers:

80, 40, 20, 10, _____

Which number comes next?

_____

Work It Out

Write About It

To solve the problem, a student might compare each number to its previous number. A student would notice that the numbers are decreasing and, upon closer look, would realize that each number is being divided by 2. After dividing the last given number by 2, the student would have the correct answer.

Looking for a Pattern is helpful when completing a function, or in-and-out, table.

Example 2

What's the Problem?

Ying needs to complete this table.

What is the missing number?

_____

Work It Out

In	Out
1	5
6	30
7	35
9	

Write About It

To solve the problem, a student might compare each "In" number to its corresponding "Out" number. A student would notice that the numbers are increasing and, upon closer look, would realize that each number is being multiplied by 5. After multiplying the last given number by 5, the student would have the correct answer.

What's the Problem?

Georgia made a necklace using 25 beads and charms. Georgia used star, heart, flower, square, and sun charms, and plain beads to make the necklace.

- Every 7th charm is a heart.
- Every 5th charm is a flower.
- Every 6th charm is a star.
- She used a square charm starting in the 3rd space and every 8th space thereafter.
- She used a sun charm starting in the 4th space and every 9th space thereafter.
- For the rest of the necklace, beads were used.

How many beads did Georgia use?_____

How many charms did Georgia use?_____

A drawing or diagram can help you "see" the problem more clearly. You can use simple pictures or symbols. Diagrams and pictures help you keep track of information in problems that take more than one step to solve.

Work It Out

Write About It

What's the Problem?

Ben is using bricks to make the outline of a giant square. Ben lays the bricks end-to-end. Each brick is 6 inches wide and 12 inches long.

How many bricks does Ben need to make a square with sides 5 feet long?

_____

 **Work It Out**

Write About It

What's the Problem?

Timothy made a pan of brownies. He cut the brownies into 3 rows with 4 brownies in each row.

How many brownies have no crispy edges, 1 crispy edge, or 2 crispy edges?

_____

_____

_____

 **Work It Out**

Write About It

What's the Problem?

Jen has a 15-inch board and some colorful nails. Jen uses a red nail at every inch, a blue nail at every $\frac{1}{2}$ inch, a green nail every $2\frac{1}{2}$ inches, and a yellow nail every 3 inches.

How many nails of each color will Jen use?

_____

_____

At which measurement will all 4 nail colors be used?

_____

REMINDER

A drawing or diagram can help you "see" the problem more clearly. You can use simple pictures or symbols. Diagrams and pictures help you keep track of information in problems that take more than one step to solve.

 **Work It Out**

Write About It

What's the Problem?

Kasey has a piece of fabric. The fabric is 36 inches long and 42 inches wide.

How many 10-inch squares can Kasey cut out of the fabric?

_____

> **REMINDER**
>
> A drawing or diagram can help you "see" the problem more clearly. You can use simple pictures or symbols. Diagrams and pictures help you keep track of information in problems that take more than one step to solve.

 **Work It Out**

Write About It

What's the Problem?

Mr. Harmony, the band teacher, had 48 pieces of licorice. He kept $\frac{1}{4}$ for himself and gave the 3 drummers equal shares of the rest of the licorice. The drummers each gave $\frac{1}{2}$ of their licorice to the 3 tuba players. The tuba players each gave $\frac{1}{3}$ of their licorice to the 3 flute players. The flute players each gave $\frac{1}{2}$ of their licorice to the 3 saxophone players.

How many pieces of licorice did each band member end up with?

A drawing or diagram can help you "see" the problem more clearly. You can use simple pictures or symbols. Diagrams and pictures help you keep track of information in problems that take more than one step to solve.

_____

_____

_____

 **Work It Out**

Write About It

What's the Problem?

Jason drew a square on a piece of paper. He divided the square into 4 equal squares. Jason then divided each square into 4 more squares of equal size.

How many squares in all?

_____

> A drawing or diagram can help you "see" the problem more clearly. You can use simple pictures or symbols. Diagrams and pictures help you keep track of information in problems that take more than one step to solve.

Work It Out

Write About It

What's the Problem?

Ollie the Octopus decides to shake hands with himself.

How many times can Ollie shake hands with himself?

_____

 **Work It Out**

Write About It

Warm-Up 9

What's the Problem?

The Romano family is meeting at a restaurant. Each square table seats 4 people, with 1 person on each side of the table. There are 16 people in the Romano family.

If the restaurant pushes the tables together in a line, how many tables will be needed to seat the family?

_____

A drawing or diagram can help you "see" the problem more clearly. You can use simple pictures or symbols. Diagrams and pictures help you keep track of information in problems that take more than one step to solve.

Work It Out

Write About It

What's the Problem?

Jared tells a secret to 3 friends. Each friend tells the secret to 3 of his or her friends. Then those friends tell the secret to 3 friends each.

Including Jared, how many people know the secret?

_____

> **REMINDER**
>
> A drawing or diagram can help you "see" the problem more clearly. You can use simple pictures or symbols. Diagrams and pictures help you keep track of information in problems that take more than one step to solve.

 Work It Out

Write About It

Warm-Up
11

What's the Problem?

Clint is making cookies using his own special recipe. He has packages of chocolate chips, chocolate candies, and walnuts. Each package contains 100 items. In his recipe, Clint uses $\frac{1}{2}$ of the chocolate chips, $\frac{1}{4}$ of the chocolate candies, and $\frac{2}{5}$ of the walnuts.

How much of each item does Clint use in his recipe?

_____

How many of each item is left?

_____

Complete the table to find out.

REMINDER

Creating a table helps you organize information.

Follow these steps:
1. Work in order and list all combinations.
2. Keep one item the same while others change.
3. Fill in any gaps.
4. Record the solution so it is easy to understand.

2 3 + 1 Work It Out 9 = 7

Item	Amount Used	Amount Unused
Chocolate Chips		
Chocolate Candies		
Walnuts		

Write About It

What's the Problem?

Mr. and Mrs. Rabbit have 6 baby rabbits. Each rabbit grows up, gets married, and has 6 baby rabbits.

How many rabbits are now in the rabbit family?

_____

The table below has been started for you. Complete the table to find out.

REMINDER

Creating a table helps you organize information.

Follow these steps:
1. Work in order and list all combinations.
2. Keep one item the same while others change.
3. Fill in any gaps.
4. Record the solution so it is easy to understand.

 **Work It Out**

Members of the Rabbit Family	Parents	Babies & Spouses	B & S Babies
Total Number of Rabbits			

Write About It

What's the Problem?

How many possible sock combinations are there given the choices below?

_____

Complete the table to find out.

- *Styles:* knee-high, ankle-high

- *Colors:* white, red

- *Designs:* dog, cat

REMINDER

Creating a table helps you organize information.

Follow these steps:
1. Work in order and list all combinations.
2. Keep one item the same while others change.
3. Fill in any gaps.
4. Record the solution so it is easy to understand.

 **Work It Out**

Style	Color	Design

Write About It

What's the Problem?

The Tooth Fairy pays $2.50 for each molar and $1.50 for each incisor. The Tooth Fairy has given Jeffrey $13.00 for fewer than 8 teeth.

How many molars and incisors has Jeffrey lost?

_____

Using the table below, try different possibilities to find the answer.

REMINDER

Creating a table helps you organize information.

Follow these steps:
1. Work in order and list all combinations.
2. Keep one item the same while others change.
3. Fill in any gaps.
4. Record the solution so it is easy to understand.

 **Work It Out**

	Number of Teeth	Amount Paid	Number of Teeth	Amount Paid	Number of Teeth	Amount Paid
Molars						
Incisors						
Total						

Write About It

What's the Problem?

Taylor delivers the newspaper to 10 customers each day. She earns 60 cents for each paper delivered on Sunday and 30 cents for each paper delivered Monday through Saturday.

How much money does Taylor earn each week?

_____

Create a table to find out.

REMINDER

Creating a table helps you organize information.

Follow these steps:
1. Work in order and list all combinations.
2. Keep one item the same while others change.
3. Fill in any gaps.
4. Record the solution so it is easy to understand.

 **Work It Out**

Write About It

What's the Problem?

How many different two-, three-, and four-digit numbers can be made using 3, 6, 8, and 1 without repeating a digit in any number?

Example: 13, 136, 1368

Create a table to find out.

Work It Out

Write About It

What's the Problem?

How many ways can $2.00 be made using 10 or fewer coins (nickels, dimes, quarters, and half-dollars)?

_____

Create a table to find out.

2 3 + 1 **Work It Out** 9 = 7

Write About It

Warm-Up 18

What's the Problem?

You have 9 bags of money worth $8.00, $9.00, $10.00, $12.00, $13.00, $14.00, $22.00, $23.00, and $24.00. You dig 9 holes in a 3-foot by 3-foot plot. You need to bury 3 bags of money in each row and column. Each row and column must equal $45.00.

Which bag will you place in each hole?

Use the table below if needed.

Work It Out

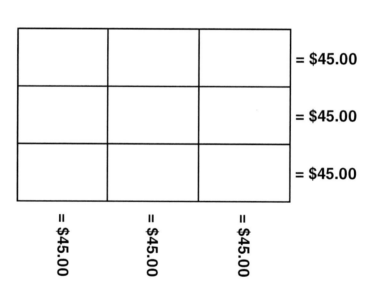

			= $45.00
			= $45.00
			= $45.00

= $45.00   = $45.00   = $45.00

Write About It

Warm-Up 19

What's the Problem?

Cynthia has blue, green, and purple pants. She also has red, orange, and yellow shirts.

How many different outfits can she make using these pieces of clothing?

_____

Create a chart showing your findings.

REMINDER

Creating a table helps you organize information.

Follow these steps:
1. Work in order and list all combinations.
2. Keep one item the same while others change.
3. Fill in any gaps.
4. Record the solution so it is easy to understand.

2 3 + 1 Work It Out 9 = 7

Write About It

What's the Problem?

Jeb weighs half as much as Corinne. Corinne weighs half as much as Ben. Together, their combined weight is 238 pounds.

How much does each person weigh?

_____

_____

_____

REMINDER

Creating a table helps you organize information.

Follow these steps:
1. Work in order and list all combinations.
2. Keep one item the same while others change.
3. Fill in any gaps.
4. Record the solution so it is easy to understand.

Work It Out

Write About It

What's the Problem?

The bus picked up 10 people each at the first 2 stops. Then 5 people got off the bus and 10 people got on. Then 9 people got off the bus and 4 people got on.

How many people are on the bus?

_____

> **REMINDER**
> Sometimes a problem is hard to visualize or to solve. Use real objects to create a model or use people (or objects) to act out the problem and its solution.
> By acting it out, talking through the problem, or using objects to represent parts of the problem, you can "see" its solution better.

 **Work It Out**

Write About It

What's the Problem?

Lindsey has 36 grapes to share evenly among herself and three friends.

How many grapes will each of them receive?

_____

REMINDER

Sometimes a problem is hard to visualize or to solve. Use real objects to create a model or use people (or objects) to act out the problem and its solution.

By acting it out, talking through the problem, or using objects to represent parts of the problem, you can "see" its solution better.

 Work It Out

Write About It

What's the Problem?

Which is more: $\frac{1}{4}$ **of** $\frac{1}{2}$ **of 64 or** $\frac{1}{3}$ **of 27?**

_____

> **REMINDER**
>
> Sometimes a problem is hard to visualize or to solve. Use real objects to create a model or use people (or objects) to act out the problem and its solution.
>
> By acting it out, talking through the problem, or using objects to represent parts of the problem, you can "see" its solution better.

 **Work It Out**

Write About It

What's the Problem?

There were 20 students equally divided into 2 teams—Red and Blue. Five Red players became Blue players, and 4 Blue players became Red players. Then 6 Red players became Blue players, and 9 Blue players became Red players.

How many students are on each team?

_____

_____

Work It Out

Write About It

What's the Problem?

Which shapes can you make using a maximum of 6 pattern block triangles?

_____

_____

Draw the shapes below.

REMINDER

Sometimes a problem is hard to visualize or to solve. Use real objects to create a model or use people (or objects) to act out the problem and its solution.

By acting it out, talking through the problem, or using objects to represent parts of the problem, you can "see" its solution better.

 **Work It Out**

Write About It

What's the Problem?

How many nickels are in a stack 1 foot high?

_____

Hint: There are 14 nickels in 1 inch.

What is the value of the nickels?

_____

> **REMINDER**
>
> Sometimes a problem is hard to visualize or to solve. Use real objects to create a model or use people (or objects) to act out the problem and its solution.
>
> By acting it out, talking through the problem, or using objects to represent parts of the problem, you can "see" its solution better.

Work It Out

Write About It

What's the Problem?

Which is worth more: a 1-inch stack of nickels or a $\frac{1}{2}$-inch stack of dimes?

_____

Hint: There are 22 dimes in 1 inch.

 **Work It Out**

Write About It

What's the Problem?

Ricky is buying candles for his mother's birthday cake. There are 8 candles in a box. Ricky buys 6 boxes of candles with 5 candles left over.

How old is Ricky's mom?

_____

  Work It Out

Write About It

What's the Problem?

The class is going on a field trip. Instead of taking a school bus, the students are being driven by their parents. Each parent can drive 4 students.

How many parent drivers are needed for the 29 students?

_____

> Sometimes a problem is hard to visualize or to solve. Use real objects to create a model or use people (or objects) to act out the problem and its solution.
> By acting it out, talking through the problem, or using objects to represent parts of the problem, you can "see" its solution better.

Work It Out

Write About It

What's the Problem?

How many crayons, laid end-to-end, will equal the perimeter of your desk?

_____

REMINDER

Sometimes a problem is hard to visualize or to solve. Use real objects to create a model or use people (or objects) to act out the problem and its solution.

By acting it out, talking through the problem, or using objects to represent parts of the problem, you can "see" its solution better.

 ## Work It Out

Write About It

What's the Problem?

The students decided to adopt a class pet. They voted on whether to adopt a bird, a snake, or a hamster. There were 22 students in the class. The bird received three times more votes than the snake and twice as many votes as the hamster.

How many votes did each animal receive?

_____

_____

_____

REMINDER

Guessing and checking helps you find reasonable guesses to solve a problem. For each guess, look at the important information presented in the problem. Check each guess against the information. Base the next guess on the previous result. (Was it too large or too small?) Recording your guesses and results in a table helps, too!

2 3 $+$ 1 **Work It Out** 9 $=$ 7

Write About It

What's the Problem?

Allen measured a window. It had a perimeter of 12 feet.

What is the length and width of the window? List the possibilities using whole numbers of feet only.

_____

_____

 Work It Out

Write About It

Warm-Up 33

What's the Problem?

Use the numbers 0, 1, 2, 3, 4, 5, 6 to make each line on the triangle have a sum of 9.

Each number can be used only one time.

REMINDER

Guessing and checking helps you find reasonable guesses to solve a problem. For each guess, look at the important information presented in the problem. Check each guess against the information. Base the next guess on the previous result. (Was it too large or too small?) Recording your guesses and results in a table helps, too!

 # Work It Out

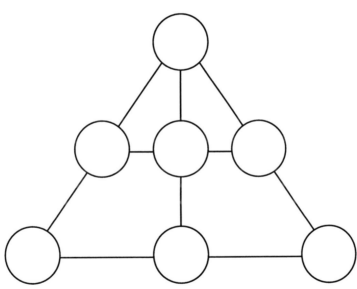

Write About It

What's the Problem?

Use the numbers 13, 14, 15, 16, 17, 18, 19, 20, and 21 to complete the table so that each row and column has a sum of 51.

Each number can be used only one time.

Work It Out

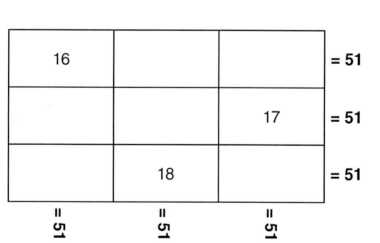

16			= 51
		17	= 51
	18		= 51
= 51	= 51	= 51	

Write About It

Warm-Up 35

What's the Problem?

Jack sells tickets to the concert. He sells twenty tickets for $70.00.

How many of each ticket type did Jack sell?

Ticket	Price
1	$5.00
Set of 2	$7.00
Set of 3	$10.00

REMINDER

Guessing and checking helps you find reasonable guesses to solve a problem. For each guess, look at the important information presented in the problem. Check each guess against the information. Base the next guess on the previous result. (Was it too large or too small?) Recording your guesses and results in a table helps, too!

 **Work It Out**

Write About It

Warm-Up 36

What's the Problem?

Mr. Souza has 8 children. He has 2 more sons than daughters.

How many sons and daughters does Mr. Souza have?

_____

_____

REMINDER

Guessing and checking helps you find reasonable guesses to solve a problem. For each guess, look at the important information presented in the problem. Check each guess against the information. Base the next guess on the previous result. (Was it too large or too small?) Recording your guesses and results in a table helps, too!

 **Work It Out**

Write About It

What's the Problem?

Raven has twice as many pockets as Sayeed and four times as many pockets as Nuha. Together, they have 21 pockets.

How many pockets does each person have?

_____

_____

_____

REMINDER

Guessing and checking helps you find reasonable guesses to solve a problem. For each guess, look at the important information presented in the problem. Check each guess against the information. Base the next guess on the previous result. (Was it too large or too small?) Recording your guesses and results in a table helps, too!

 **Work It Out**

Write About It

What's the Problem?

The students at Great Expectations Elementary School wear uniforms. The girls' shirts have 5 buttons on them, and the boys' shirts have 3 buttons on them. In Ms. McRae's class, there is a total of 78 buttons. There are more boys than girls in her class. However, the girl button total is higher than the boy button total.

How many boys and girls are in Ms. McRae's class?

_____

_____

REMINDER

Guessing and checking helps you find reasonable guesses to solve a problem. For each guess, look at the important information presented in the problem. Check each guess against the information. Base the next guess on the previous result. (Was it too large or too small?) Recording your guesses and results in a table helps, too!

2 $3 + 1$ **Work It Out** $9 = 7$

Write About It

What's the Problem?

Sidney needs to mail a package.

Can Sidney make $2.40 in postage using only 18-cent stamps and 33-cent stamps? How?

_____

_____

REMINDER

Guessing and checking helps you find reasonable guesses to solve a problem. For each guess, look at the important information presented in the problem. Check each guess against the information. Base the next guess on the previous result. (Was it too large or too small?) Recording your guesses and results in a table helps, too!

2 3 + 1 **Work It Out** 9 = 7

Write About It

What's the Problem?

Take 2 pieces of 9-inch by 12-inch construction paper. Roll 1 into a tall cylinder and 1 into a short cylinder. Each cylinder has a 1-inch overlap.

Which cylinder holds more counters?

_____

 Work It Out

Write About It

Warm-Up 41

What's the Problem?

Thomas collects cans for recycling. One day, Thomas collects 1 can. The next day, he collects 4 cans. On the third day, he collects 8 cans, and on the fourth day, he collects 13 cans.

How many cans will Thomas collect on the tenth day?

_____

> **REMINDER**
>
> Looking for a pattern makes it easier to predict what comes next. In a problem, study any number pattern to see how the numbers change from one number to the next. For example, to find the rule for the pattern 2, 4, 8, 16, study how 2 and 4, 4 and 8, etc., are related. You will see that each number is double (2 times) the number before it.

 Work It Out

Write About It

What's the Problem?

What is the rule for the number machine?

_____

2 3 + 1 Work It Out 9 = 7

In	Out
10	30
8	24
14	42

Write About It

54

What's the Problem?

If the 2 numbers in a two-digit number are added together, which sum is the most common?

_____

Note: There may be more than one answer.

 # Work It Out

1	2	3	4	5	6	7	8	9	10
11	12	13	14	15	16	17	18	19	20
21	22	23	24	25	26	27	28	29	30
31	32	33	34	35	36	37	38	39	40
41	42	43	44	45	46	47	48	49	50
51	52	53	54	55	56	57	58	59	60
61	62	63	64	65	66	67	68	69	70
71	72	73	74	75	76	77	78	79	80
81	82	83	84	85	86	87	88	89	90
91	92	93	94	95	96	97	98	99	100

Write About It

What's the Problem?

For 10 days, Tony had animals delivered to his farm. He received sheep, mice, pigs, goats, horses, cows, chickens, roosters, cats, and donkeys.

- On day one, Tony received 1 sheep.

- On day two, Tony received 2 mice and 1 sheep.

- On day three, Tony received 3 pigs, 2 mice, and 1 sheep.

If the pattern continues, how many of each animal will Tony receive in all after 10 days of deliveries? Create a table if needed.

Which animal(s) will there be the most of?

_____

Work It Out

Write About It

What's the Problem?

Lettie has been getting into shape. On Sunday, she did 1 chin-up. On Monday, she did 2 chin-ups. On Tuesday, she did 4 chin-ups, and on Wednesday she did 7 chin-ups. Lettie continues to do chin-ups for the rest of the week.

If Lettie continues the pattern, how many chin-ups will she do on Thursday, Friday, and Saturday?

_____

_____

_____

Looking for a pattern makes it easier to predict what comes next. In a problem, study any number pattern to see how the numbers change from one number to the next. For example, to find the rule for the pattern 2, 4, 8, 16, study how 2 and 4, 4 and 8, etc., are related. You will see that each number is double (2 times) the number before it.

Work It Out

Write About It

Warm-Up
46

What's the Problem?

A machine can punch 3 holes every 5 seconds.

How many holes are punched after 1 minute?

_____

REMINDER

Looking for a pattern makes it easier to predict what comes next. In a problem, study any number pattern to see how the numbers change from one number to the next. For example, to find the rule for the pattern 2, 4, 8, 16, study how 2 and 4, 4 and 8, etc., are related. You will see that each number is double (2 times) the number before it.

Work It Out

Write About It

What's the Problem?

100, 88, 91, 79, 82, 70, 73, 61, 64, _____, _____, _____

What are the next 3 numbers in the pattern?

_____

Will the pattern ever reach an even 0?

_____

Looking for a pattern makes it easier to predict what comes next. In a problem, study any number pattern to see how the numbers change from one number to the next. For example, to find the rule for the pattern 2, 4, 8, 16, study how 2 and 4, 4 and 8, etc., are related. You will see that each number is double (2 times) the number before it.

Work It Out

Write About It

What's the Problem?

How much would $10.00 in American money be worth in Canadian dollars?

_____

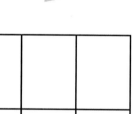
 **Work It Out**

American Money	$1.00	$2.00	$3.00						
Canadian Money	$1.05	$2.10	$3.15						

Write About It

What's the Problem?

The baby elephant grows at a tremendous rate. At one day old, it ate 100 peanuts. On day two, it ate 225 peanuts. On day three, it ate 375 peanuts. On day four, it ate 550 peanuts.

If the elephant continues to eat at this rate, how many peanuts will it eat on day seven?

_____

> **REMINDER**
>
> Looking for a pattern makes it easier to predict what comes next. In a problem, study any number pattern to see how the numbers change from one number to the next. For example, to find the rule for the pattern 2, 4, 8, 16, study how 2 and 4, 4 and 8, etc., are related. You will see that each number is double (2 times) the number before it.

Work It Out

Write About It

What's the Problem?

The students are given markers. One student is given 4 markers, two students share 8 markers, and three students share 12 markers.

How many markers would 6 students share?

_____

REMINDER

Looking for a pattern makes it easier to predict what comes next. In a problem, study any number pattern to see how the numbers change from one number to the next. For example, to find the rule for the pattern 2, 4, 8, 16, study how 2 and 4, 4 and 8, etc., are related. You will see that each number is double (2 times) the number before it.

Work It Out

Write About It

What's the Problem?

Work It Out

Arlo has two dozen muffins. He sells
$\frac{2}{3}$ of the muffins for 25 cents each.
He sells the remaining muffins for 10
cents each.

How much money does Arlo make?

_____

**What is the average selling price
for the muffins?**

_____

WRITE
ABOUT IT

_____

_____

· ·

What's the Problem?

Work It Out

Martha sells cookies for 25 cents,
milk for 10 cents, or cookies and milk
for 30 cents.

**If 4 people buy cookies, 3 people
buy milk, and 3 people buy both
milk and cookies, how much
money will Martha earn?**

_____

WRITE
ABOUT IT

_____

_____

What's the Problem?

Work It Out

Mr. Newcastle built 5 new schools. Each school had 18 doors and 39 windows.

How many doors and windows in all?

_____

WRITE ABOUT IT

_____

_____

Warm-Up 54

What's the Problem?

Work It Out

In the 5 new schools that Mr. Newcastle built, he used special door hinges. Each door required 3 hinges.

Since each school has 18 doors, how many hinges did Mr. Newcastle need?

_____

WRITE ABOUT IT

_____

_____

Warm-Up 55

What's the Problem?

Work It Out

Using three 3s in each math problem and no other numbers, list the different sums and differences you can make.

Example: 33 + 3 = 36, 33 − 3 = 30

_____

_____

_____

WRITE ABOUT IT

_____

_____

- -

Warm-Up 56

What's the Problem?

Work It Out

Jessica needs to make math problems with solutions of 0 through 10. She must use 3 different single-digit numbers in each problem. She can add, subtract, multiply, and/or divide the numbers.

What math problems can Jessica make?

_____

_____

WRITE ABOUT IT

_____

_____

What's the Problem?

Work It Out

There are 500 gumballs in the gumball machine. Half of the gumballs are red, $\frac{1}{5}$ are blue, $\frac{1}{10}$ are yellow, and the rest are green. Shelly takes out $\frac{1}{2}$ of the red gumballs and replaces them with the same amount of yellow gumballs.

How many gumballs of each color are in the machine?

WRITE ABOUT IT

What's the Problem?

Work It Out

Maggie has 100 gumballs. She keeps $\frac{1}{2}$ for herself and gives $\frac{1}{2}$ to her brother, Scott. Scott keeps 10 for himself and divides the remaining gumballs evenly between his 2 friends, Bailey and Spencer. Spencer keeps $\frac{1}{2}$ for himself and gives the rest to his sister, Sally.

How many gumballs does each person have?

WRITE ABOUT IT

What's the Problem?

Work It Out

You are working for 4 weeks.

Would you rather be paid $5.00 a week or be paid $1.75 the first week and have the amount doubled each week? Why?

_____

_____

_____

WRITE ABOUT IT

_____

_____

· ·

Warm-Up 60

What's the Problem?

Work It Out

Jim is busy stacking cups on the shelves. He will be paid 3 cents for the first cup, 6 cents for the second cup, and 12 cents for the third cup.

If the pattern continues, how much will Jim be paid for the tenth cup?

_____

How much money will Jim earn in all?

_____

WRITE ABOUT IT

_____

Warm-Up 61

What's the Problem?

Work It Out

Antonio is trying to become a speed typist. He typed his 144-word state report in 8 minutes.

How many words per minute did Antonio type?

_____

WRITE ABOUT IT

_____

_____

Warm-Up 62

What's the Problem?

Work It Out

Antonio worked on his typing speed. This time, he typed his 160-word book report in 10 minutes.

How many words per minute did Antonio type this time?

_____

Did his speed improve?

_____

WRITE ABOUT IT

_____

Warm-Up 63

What's the Problem?

Levi carves and paints people's names out of wood. Each name is made using capital letters.

How much would it cost to have Levi make your name?

_____

WRITE ABOUT IT

Work It Out

Letter	Rate
A, E, F, H, I, K, L, M, N, T, V, W, X, Y, Z	$0.38
B, D, J, P, Q, R, U	$0.72
C, G, O, S	$1.04

_____

Warm-Up 64

What's the Problem?

Levi is offering a special deal! This time all the vowels in your name are free!

How much would your name cost now?

_____

What is the difference between the price now and the price before?

_____

WRITE ABOUT IT

Work It Out

What's the Problem? Work It Out

Garth is paid to number pages in a book.

How much will he earn to number a 100-page book?

_____

Pages	Rate
First 10 pages	1 cent per page
Next 15 pages	2 cents per page
Next 35 pages	3 cents per page
Remaining pages	4 cents per page

WRITE ABOUT IT

_____

_____

Warm-Up 66

What's the Problem? Work It Out

Betty is paid for numbering paint cans at the hardware store.

How many times will Betty write the digit 1 when writing the numbers 1 through 100?

_____

WRITE ABOUT IT

_____

What's the Problem?

Work It Out

Ben, Pat, and Keith are standing in a line. They are passing a ball up and down the line. Ben hands the ball to Pat, and Pat passes the ball to Keith. Then Keith passes the ball to Pat, and Pat passes it back to Ben.

Starting with Ben, how many times will each person touch the ball if it is passed a total of 11 times?

WRITE
ABOUT IT

What's the Problem?

Work It Out

Chris tosses a Frisbee to Chuck, and Chuck tosses it back. Then Chris tosses the Frisbee to Alicia, and Alicia tosses it back.

How many times will each person throw the Frisbee if it is tossed in this pattern a total of 10 times?

WRITE
ABOUT IT

Warm-Up 69

What's the Problem?

Work It Out

Connie received $100 for her birthday. She spent $\frac{1}{20}$ of the money on a puzzle, $\frac{1}{5}$ of it on a pair of sneakers, $\frac{1}{4}$ of it on a new bike, and $\frac{1}{10}$ of it went into her piggy bank. She put the rest of the money into her college savings account.

How much money did she save for college?

_____

WRITE ABOUT IT

_____

_____

Warm-Up 70

What's the Problem?

Work It Out

Pete had a bag of trail mix. The bag contained 100 pieces of walnuts, almonds, raisins, and chocolate. The mix was 10% chocolate, 40% almonds, and the rest was evenly divided between walnuts and raisins.

How many walnuts and raisins were in the bag?

_____

_____

WRITE ABOUT IT

_____

_____

What's the Problem?

Dana has $35.00 to spend each month on her cell phone.

Which items can Dana get? List one combination.

_____

_____

_____

WRITE ABOUT IT

Work It Out

Item	Monthly Rate
Cell phone with 50 free min.	$13.99
Cell phone with 100 free min.	$17.99
Unlimited e-mail	$7.84
Unlimited texting	$6.38
Gaming (one hour)	$4.75
Unlimited gaming	$10.00
Ringtones (ten per month)	$ 9.90
Unlimited ringtones	$14.25

_____

Warm-Up 72

What's the Problem?

Nigel was very careful with his cell phone usage. This month, his bill was the lowest ever. He used 10 minutes of peak time and 25 minutes of non-peak time. Nigel also had 100 text messages and downloaded 15 ringtones.

What was the total amount of Nigel's cell phone bill?

_____

WRITE ABOUT IT

Work It Out

Item	Rate
Calls made during peak time	18 cents per minute
Calls made during non-peak time	10 cents per minute
Text messages	3 cents each
Ringtones	20 cents each

_____

What's the Problem?

Work It Out

Name 4 different ways that the number 789 can be represented.

_____

_____

_____

_____

WRITE ABOUT IT

_____

_____

What's the Problem?

Work It Out

Name 4 different ways that the number 1,263 can be represented.

_____

_____

_____

_____

WRITE ABOUT IT

_____

_____

What's the Problem?

Work It Out

Billy is having a barbecue. Buns are sold 10 to a bag. Hot dogs are sold 8 to a pack.

What is the fewest number of bags of hot-dog buns and packs of hot dogs that Billy will need to buy so that each hot dog has a bun with no buns left over?

_____

_____

WRITE ABOUT IT

- -

What's the Problem?

Work It Out

Wilma is grilling beef hamburger patties at the barbecue. Each pound of beef can make 4 patties. There are 8 hamburger buns in a bag.

If Wilma needs to make 24 hamburgers, how many bags of hamburger buns and how many pounds of beef will she need?

_____

_____

WRITE ABOUT IT

What's the Problem?

Work It Out

In July, Amy put $10.00 in her new savings account. In August, she put $10.50 in her account and in September, she put $12.50 in her account.

How much money does Amy now have in her account?

_____

> **WRITE ABOUT IT**

_____

_____

What's the Problem?

Work It Out

Ross is saving for a scooter. The scooter costs $225.00.

If Ross saves $5.00 each week, how many weeks will it take until he has enough money to buy the scooter?

_____

> **WRITE ABOUT IT**

_____

_____

What's the Problem?

Work It Out

Lawrence started a new book. He read 30 pages on Monday night, 45 pages on Tuesday night, and 89 pages on Wednesday night.

If the book has 300 pages, how many pages does Lawrence have left to read?

_____

WRITE ABOUT IT

_____

_____

What's the Problem?

Work It Out

There are 85 children in the after-school program. Each child gets 3 carrots at snack time.

How many carrots are needed for all of the children?

_____

WRITE ABOUT IT

_____

What's the Problem?

Work It Out

Lampley and Claremont are two small towns. The populations of the two towns are 2,401 and 2,843.

If 25% of the total population is children, how many adults live in the two towns?

_____

> **WRITE ABOUT IT**

_____

_____

What's the Problem?

Work It Out

Sweet Water Valley has a population of 2,500 citizens: 40% are adults, 10% are newborns, and the rest are children and teenagers.

How many citizens are in each population group?

_____

_____

_____

> **WRITE ABOUT IT**

_____

_____

What's the Problem?

Work It Out

Caterina has 18 books. Anissa has three times as many books as her sister, Caterina.

How many books does Anissa have?

_____

How many books do the sisters have in all?

_____

WRITE ABOUT IT

_____

_____

What's the Problem?

Work It Out

There are 526 cows on the range. Each cow needs 3 acres of land to feed on.

How many total acres of land does the farmer need?

_____

WRITE ABOUT IT

_____

_____

What's the Problem?   Work It Out

Jamie emptied the coins out of his piggy bank. When he sorted the coins, Jamie counted 25 quarters.

How many dollars does he have?

_____

WRITE ABOUT IT

_____

_____

· ·

What's the Problem?   Work It Out

Nancy has $45.00. She goes shopping and picks out a dress for $12.00, a blouse for $15.00, and new shoes for $25.00.

Does Nancy have enough money to pay for these items?

_____

How much money does she have left over (or how much more money does Nancy need)?

_____

WRITE ABOUT IT

_____

What's the Problem?

Work It Out

Brianna belongs to Scout Troop #251. There are 30 kids in Brianna's troop. Forty percent of the kids are 8 years old. The rest are 9 years old.

How many kids are 9 years old?

_____

How many are 8 years old?

_____

WRITE ABOUT IT

_____

_____

· ·

Warm-Up 88

What's the Problem?

Work It Out

At the beginning of each hockey season, Harris buys a new pair of ice skates. His new pair of ice skates this year were originally priced at $56.00, but now they are 20% off.

How much will Harris pay for the new ice skates?

_____

WRITE ABOUT IT

_____

What's the Problem?

Bill had a bag of candy. On Monday, he ate $\frac{1}{2}$ of the candy. On Tuesday, he ate $\frac{1}{4}$ of the candy. On Wednesday, he ate $\frac{1}{8}$, or 2 pieces, of the candy.

How many candies were in the bag?

_____

How many candies did he eat each day? How many candies are left?

_____

Work It Out

WRITE
ABOUT IT

_____

_____

What's the Problem?

Three girls bought a pizza for lunch. One girl ate $\frac{1}{3}$ of the pizza, another girl ate $\frac{1}{4}$ of the pizza, and the third girl ate the rest of the pizza.

How much of the pizza did the third girl eat?

_____

Work It Out

WRITE
ABOUT IT

_____

What's the Problem?

Work It Out

Chess is played on a square board with 8 rows and 8 columns. The pawn begins in the second row. On its first move, it can move either 1 space or 2 spaces. After that, the pawn can only move 1 space at a time. The knight (or horse) begins in the last row. It can move up 2 spaces and sideways 1 space, or it can move up 1 space or sideways 2 spaces.

Which piece can get to the other side of the board using the fewest moves?

WRITE ABOUT IT

What's the Problem?

Work It Out

The bishop and king are 2 other pieces on the chessboard. They are both in the back row of the game board. The bishop is in the third space from the left or the right. The king is in the fifth space from the left. The bishop can only move diagonally. It can move 1 space or many spaces each move. The spaces have to be touching. The king can move in any direction but only 1 space at a time.

Which piece can get to the other side of the board using the fewest moves?

WRITE ABOUT IT

What's the Problem?　　　　Work It Out

If 5 toothpicks are used to make 2 triangles, how many toothpicks are needed to make 7 triangles?

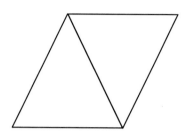

WRITE ABOUT IT

Warm-Up 94

What's the Problem?　　　　Work It Out

It takes 4 toothpicks to make 1 square.

Using the fewest number of toothpicks, make 4 squares.

How many toothpicks did you use?

WRITE ABOUT IT

Warm-Up 95

What's the Problem?

Work It Out

Chase drew a triangle. The length of each side of the triangle is 8 cm, 7 cm, and 12 cm.

What is the perimeter of the triangle Chase drew?

_____

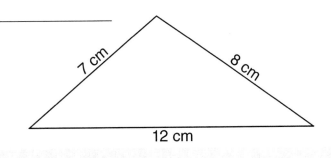

WRITE ABOUT IT

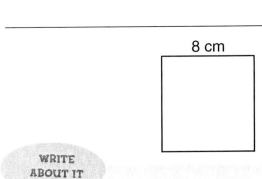

Warm-Up 96

What's the Problem?

Work It Out

Janie drew a square. Each side of the square was 8 cm long.

What is the perimeter of the square Janie made?

WRITE ABOUT IT

Warm-Up 97

What's the Problem?

Work It Out

Sonya made a rectangle. The short sides are 4 inches long and the long sides are 6 inches long.

Draw the rectangle Sonya made.

What is the perimeter?

_____

WRITE ABOUT IT

_____

_____

Warm-Up 98

What's the Problem?

Work It Out

Tim made the trapezoid shown below.

What is the perimeter?

_____

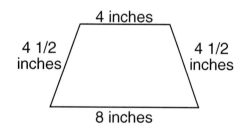

4 inches

4 1/2 inches

4 1/2 inches

8 inches

WRITE ABOUT IT

_____

What's the Problem?

Work It Out

Diane arranged the blocks in the pattern shown below.

What is the total area?

_____

What is the total perimeter?

_____

☐ = 1 square unit

WRITE ABOUT IT

_____

_____

- -

Warm-Up 100

What's the Problem?

Work It Out

Journey drew a shape with an area of 12 square units.

What shape did Journey make?

_____

What is its perimeter?

_____

WRITE ABOUT IT

_____

_____

What's the Problem?

Work It Out

Ethan drew some squares to make this grid.

What is the area of the grid?

_____

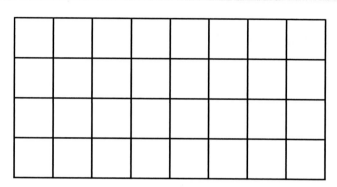

> **WRITE ABOUT IT**

_____

_____

What's the Problem?

Work It Out

Jon drew some squares to make this grid.

What is the area of the grid?

_____

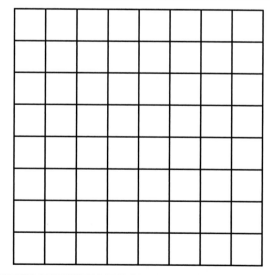

> **WRITE ABOUT IT**

_____

_____

Warm-Up 103

What's the Problem?

Work It Out

Write the numbers 0 through 9. Draw a line of symmetry for each number.

Which numbers are symmetrical?

_____

_____

_____

> WRITE ABOUT IT

_____

_____

Warm-Up 104

What's the Problem?

Work It Out

Write the letters of the alphabet in capital letters. Draw a line of symmetry for each letter.

Which letters are symmetrical?

_____

_____

_____

> WRITE ABOUT IT

_____

What's the Problem?

Work It Out

Lois had to make as many different 4-sided shapes as possible.

Which shapes could Lois have made?

_____

_____

Draw and label each shape.

WRITE
ABOUT IT

_____

_____

- -

What's the Problem?

Work It Out

Clark had to make many different shapes with 5 or more sides.

Which shapes could Clark have made?

_____

_____

Draw and label each shape.

WRITE
ABOUT IT

_____

_____

What's the Problem?

Frank made a design using 3 different shapes. Then he transformed it by sliding, flipping, reflecting, or turning it.

What would the design look like if Frank did 2 different transformations on it?

Work It Out

WRITE ABOUT IT

_____

_____

• •

Warm-Up
108

What's the Problem?

Make a design using at least 3 different shapes.

Draw the shape after it has been transformed 2 times.

Describe the transformations.

Work It Out

_____

_____

_____

WRITE ABOUT IT

_____

Geometry: shape composition and decomposition, pattern blocks

What's the Problem?

Work It Out

Rita made this shape using pattern blocks.

List the different triangles, trapezoids, rhombi, and hexagons you can identify from Rita's shape.

Use the numbers to show which blocks you would use.

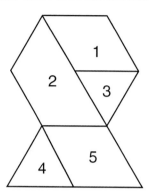

_____

_____

WRITE
ABOUT IT

_____

_____

• •

What's the Problem?

Work It Out

Lola made this shape using pattern blocks.

List the different triangles, trapezoids, rhombi, and hexagons you can identify from Lola's shape.

Use the numbers to show which blocks you would use.

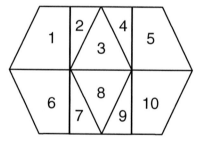

_____

_____

WRITE
ABOUT IT

_____

What's the Problem?

Work It Out

Georgia wants to create a border for her bedroom.

Using pattern blocks, design a pattern for Georgia.

WRITE ABOUT IT

What's the Problem?

Work It Out

Georgia also wants to make a border for her kitchen. She wants to use the same blocks as the ones she used for her bedroom border.

What other border could Georgia make using the same pattern blocks?

WRITE ABOUT IT

What's the Problem?

Work It Out

Stacy made 6 different shapes. She made a circle, a square, a rectangle, a pentagon, an octagon, and an oval.

What are the different ways Stacy could sort the shapes?

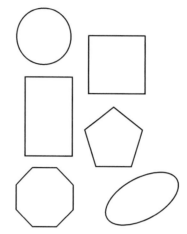

_____

_____

_____

WRITE ABOUT IT

_____

_____

Warm-Up 114

What's the Problem?

Work It Out

Reba had 1 of each pattern block shown.

What are the different ways Reba could sort them?

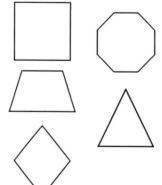

_____

_____

_____

WRITE ABOUT IT

_____

Warm-Up 115

What's the Problem?

Bobby was stacking his 6 games and activities on a shelf.

- The chess set was at the bottom of the stack.
- The cards were on top of the marbles.
- The marbles were on top of the blocks.
- The coloring books were beneath the blocks.
- The checkers were above the cards.

Where was each game located?

WRITE ABOUT IT

Work It Out

Top _____

_____

_____

_____

_____

Bottom _____

Warm-Up 116

What's the Problem?

Debbie put her 6 crayons neatly back in the box.

- The yellow crayon was third, and the purple crayon was last.
- The green crayon was after the yellow crayon but before the blue crayon.
- The orange crayon was second.
- The red crayon was before the orange crayon.

What was the order of the crayons?

WRITE ABOUT IT

Work It Out

1st _____

2nd _____

3rd _____

4th _____

5th _____

6th _____

What's the Problem?

Work It Out

Jeremy made a hexagon. Using 2 lines, he divided it into 3 different shapes.

Which shapes did Jeremy make?

_____

_____

WRITE
ABOUT IT

_____

_____

What's the Problem?

Work It Out

Renee made a rectangle. She used 2 lines to make 1 square and 2 triangles.

How did Renee divide the rectangle?

_____

_____

_____

WRITE
ABOUT IT

_____

What's the Problem?

Work It Out

Katie has 4 triangles and 1 rectangle.

What solid shape can she make?

_____

How many corners will it have?

_____

WRITE ABOUT IT

_____

_____

What's the Problem?

Work It Out

Cassie has 2 triangles and 3 rectangles.

What solid shape can she make?

_____

How many corners will it have?

_____

WRITE ABOUT IT

_____

_____

What's the Problem?

Work It Out

Sandra has a square. She needs to divide it into 4 equal parts.

How many different ways can Sandra do this?

_____

WRITE ABOUT IT

_____

_____

Warm-Up 122

What's the Problem?

Work It Out

Charles has a hexagon. He needs to divide it into 4 equal parts.

How many different ways can Charles do this?

_____

WRITE ABOUT IT

_____

_____

What's the Problem?

Work It Out

Rita has only trapezoids.

Which other pattern block shapes can she make using only trapezoids?

_____

_____

_____

_____

_____

What's the Problem?

Work It Out

Ari has only rhombi.

Which other pattern block shapes can he make using only rhombi?

_____

_____

_____

_____

Geometry: shape composition, tangrams

What's the Problem?   Work It Out

Seth has a tangram that he cut up into individual shapes.

Using 2 or more of the tangram shapes, how many different triangles can he make? List or draw them.

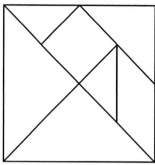

_____

_____

_____

WRITE ABOUT IT

_____

- -

What's the Problem?   Work It Out

Sharon has a tangram that she cut up into individual shapes.

Using 2 or more of the tangram shapes, how many different squares can she make? List or draw them.

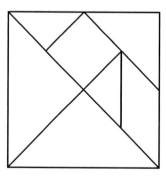

_____

_____

_____

WRITE ABOUT IT

_____

What's the Problem?

Ira was using his geoboard to make different shapes. He made a shape with an area of 25 (36 pegs).

What shape did he make?

_____

What is the perimeter?

_____

WRITE ABOUT IT

Work It Out

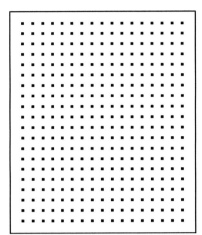

What's the Problem?

Shelly was using her geoboard to make different shapes. She made a shape with an area of 20.

What shape did she make?

_____

What is the perimeter?

_____

WRITE ABOUT IT

Work It Out

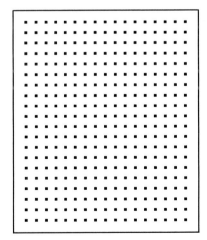

What's the Problem?

Work It Out

Tyrone is trying to make a pattern for a cube.

What should the pattern look like?

WRITE
ABOUT IT

_____

_____

What's the Problem?

Work It Out

Lucy is trying to make a pattern for a triangular pyramid.

What should the pattern look like?

WRITE
ABOUT IT

_____

Geometry: geometric solids, patterns

What's the Problem?

Work It Out

Mr. Clark's class is taking a field trip to the aquarium. The bus leaves at 5:45 a.m. and returns at 7:15 p.m.

How long is the field trip?

_____

WRITE ABOUT IT

_____

_____

What's the Problem?

Work It Out

The school's relay race record is 5 minutes. This year's team had times shown on the chart.

Did this year's team beat the school record?

_____

Racer	Time
Ana	58 seconds
Bea	47 seconds
Cruz	61 seconds
Dan	86 seconds

WRITE ABOUT IT

_____

_____

Warm-Up 133

What's the Problem?   **Work It Out**

The temperature is 30°C. Julia doesn't know whether she should wear a heavy jacket.

What is the temperature in Fahrenheit degrees?

Formula: $°C \times \dfrac{9}{5} + 32 = °F$

_____

Does Julia need a heavy jacket?

_____

WRITE ABOUT IT

Warm-Up 134

What's the Problem?   **Work It Out**

In January, the average high temperature was 62°F; in February, it was 65°F; and in March, it was 68°F.

What was the average temperature for these 3 months?

_____

WRITE ABOUT IT

What's the Problem?

Work It Out

Benjamin planted some beans in his garden. It takes 80 days for a bean seed to grow big enough to be harvested.

How many weeks and days is that?

_____

_____

WRITE
ABOUT IT

_____

_____

. . . .

Warm-Up
136

What's the Problem?

Work It Out

Johanna was born on Leap Day, February 29, 2000.

How many actual birthdays will Johanna have by the end of 2020?

_____

WRITE
ABOUT IT

_____

_____

Measurement: addition, decimals, division, average

What's the Problem?

Work It Out

Jimmy ran 0.6 of a mile on Tuesday. On Wednesday, he ran 1.1 miles and on Thursday, he ran 0.8 of a mile.

How many miles did Jimmy run in all?

_____

WRITE
ABOUT IT

_____

_____

- -

Warm-Up
138

What's the Problem?

Work It Out

Helen loves to ride her bike. On Monday, she rode her bike for 15 miles. On Tuesday, she rode her bike for 12 miles. And on Wednesday, she rode her bike for 13 miles.

What is the average number of miles per day that Helen rode her bike?

_____

WRITE
ABOUT IT

_____

_____

What's the Problem?

Work It Out

Each morning, Woodward Elementary has recess. The recess begins at 10:50 a.m. and lasts for 20 minutes.

What time will recess be over?

_____

WRITE
ABOUT IT

_____

_____

What's the Problem?

Work It Out

On Tuesday evenings, Marty watches his favorite television program. The television program is $1\frac{1}{2}$ hours long. It is over at 9:15 p.m.

What time did the program begin?

_____

WRITE
ABOUT IT

_____

_____

What's the Problem?

Work It Out

Zach and Barry are best friends.

Zach is 5 feet tall. Barry is $4\frac{1}{3}$ feet tall.

How many inches taller is Zach than Barry?

_____

WRITE
ABOUT IT

_____

_____

What's the Problem?

Work It Out

Martha wants to make a blanket for her dog. She has a piece of material that is 24 inches by 48 inches. She wants to make a blanket that is $1\frac{1}{2}$ feet by $4\frac{1}{2}$ feet.

Does Martha have enough material?

_____

WRITE
ABOUT IT

_____

_____

What's the Problem?

Work It Out

Sylvia buys a yard of fabric. One yard is 36 inches.

How many inches would 6 yards be?

_____

WRITE ABOUT IT

_____

_____

What's the Problem?

Work It Out

Steven has to chalk the lines on the football field. The football field is 100 yards long.

How many feet is that?

_____

How many inches is that?

_____

WRITE ABOUT IT

_____

_____

What's the Problem?

Work It Out

Kelly is studying the metric system. Kelly knows that there are 1,000 meters in 1 kilometer.

How many meters are in 10 kilometers?

_____

WRITE
ABOUT IT

_____

_____

What's the Problem?

Work It Out

Cheryl knows that 1 inch is equal to 2.54 centimeters.

How many centimeters are in 1 foot?

_____

WRITE
ABOUT IT

_____

What's the Problem?

Work It Out

There are 60 seconds in 1 minute, 60 minutes in 1 hour, and 24 hours in 1 day.

How many minutes are there in 1 day?

_____

How many seconds are there in 1 day?

_____

WRITE
ABOUT IT

_____

_____

• •

What's the Problem?

Work It Out

There are 365 days in a year.

How many days are there in 3 years?

_____

WRITE
ABOUT IT

_____

What's the Problem?

Work It Out

Toby weighed a bag of hot-dog buns. A 1-pound bag of hot-dog buns contains 8 buns.

How many buns in 12 pounds?

_____

WRITE
ABOUT IT

_____

_____

Warm-Up
150

What's the Problem?

Work It Out

In England, people are weighed in stones. One stone is equal to 14 pounds.

If Tyler weighs 8 stones, how many pounds is that?

_____

WRITE
ABOUT IT

_____

_____

What's the Problem?

Work It Out

Sage's birthday is in 2 weeks.

How many more days are there until his birthday party?

_____

WRITE
ABOUT IT

_____

_____

· ·

Warm-Up
152

What's the Problem?

Work It Out

June is counting the days until summer vacation, which begins June 1.

If today is October 1, how many more days are there until summer vacation?

_____

WRITE
ABOUT IT

_____

What's the Problem?

Work It Out

Danielle and David are twins. They were born 12 minutes apart. Danielle was born first at 11:57 a.m.

What time was David born?

_____

_____

• •

What's the Problem?

Work It Out

Jane goes to school 6 hours a day (Monday–Friday) for 36 weeks.

How many hours does Jane spend in school?

_____

WRITE ABOUT IT

_____

What's the Problem?

Work It Out

Jordan spent 55 minutes driving from Visalia to the Fresno airport. He then flew for 1 hour and 55 minutes to San Francisco, had a 1 hour and 40 minute layover, and then flew for 3 hours and 59 minutes to Houston. Jordan then had a 20-minute drive home.

How many hours and minutes did it take Jordan to go from Visalia to his home in Houston?

WRITE ABOUT IT

• •

What's the Problem?

Work It Out

Before eating dinner, Beverly spends 40 minutes doing her homework and then spends 35 minutes practicing the piano.

If Beverly eats dinner at 6:30 p.m., what time does she start her homework?

WRITE ABOUT IT

Warm-Up 157

What's the Problem?

Work It Out

Kari swam for 28 minutes, 34 minutes, and 46 minutes.

How many hours and minutes did Kari swim in all?

_____

_____

WRITE ABOUT IT

_____

_____

• •

Warm-Up 158

What's the Problem?

Work It Out

Jason reads his library book 4 nights each week. On two nights, he read for 23 minutes each. One night, he read for 18 minutes, and on another night he read for 15 minutes.

How many hours and minutes did Jason read in all?

_____

_____

WRITE ABOUT IT

_____

_____

What's the Problem?

Work It Out

People should drink eight 8-ounce glasses of water each day.

Note: 16 ounces = 1 pint;
2 pints = 1 quart

How many pints is that?

_____

How many quarts is that?

_____

WRITE
ABOUT IT

_____

_____

What's the Problem?

Work It Out

Bruce bought a gallon of milk. There are 16 cups in a gallon. There are 8 ounces in each cup.

How many ounces are in 1 gallon of milk?

_____

WRITE
ABOUT IT

_____

Warm-Up 161

What's the Problem?

Work It Out

Ellen visits a new state each day.

How many weeks and days will it take Ellen to visit all 50 states?

_____

_____

WRITE ABOUT IT

_____

_____

Warm-Up 162

What's the Problem?

Work It Out

The Plymale family will be taking a long cruise. They will be gone for 5 weeks and 3 days.

How many days in all will the family be gone?

_____

WRITE ABOUT IT

_____

_____

What's the Problem?

Work It Out

Allison had a board. The board was 2 feet long. She cut the board in half. Allison then took one of the halves and cut it in half. Finally, Allison took one of the new halves and cut it in half again.

How many boards does Allison now have?

_____

How many inches long is each board?

_____

WRITE ABOUT IT

_____

_____

. . . .

Warm-Up 164

What's the Problem?

Work It Out

Brandy measured his room. It measured 12 feet by 15 feet.

How many yards wide and long is Brady's room?

Note: 3 feet = 1 yard

_____

WRITE ABOUT IT

_____

_____

What's the Problem?

Work It Out

Lila used a meter stick to measure the length of the fence. The fence was 20 meters long.

How many yards is that?

Note: Multiply the number of meters by 1.09 to get the number of yards.

_____

> **WRITE ABOUT IT**

_____

_____

What's the Problem?

Work It Out

Darby is 5 feet, 3 inches tall.

How many centimeters is that?

Note: 1 inch = 2.54 centimeters

_____

> **WRITE ABOUT IT**

_____

What's the Problem?

Work It Out

Quita has a box with sides that measure 8 inches long. All the sides are the same length.

What is the volume of the box?

Note: Volume = length x width x height

_____

WRITE ABOUT IT

_____

_____

- -

Warm-Up 168

What's the Problem?

Work It Out

Hubert has a shoebox. It is 5 inches long, 4 inches high, and 3 inches wide.

What is the volume of the shoebox?

Note: Volume = length x width x height

_____

WRITE ABOUT IT

_____

_____

Warm-Up 169

What's the Problem?

Work It Out

Monty is building a house. Each window has an area of 24 feet.

What are the possible lengths and widths of Monty's windows?

_____

_____

_____

_____

WRITE ABOUT IT

_____

_____

Warm-Up 170

What's the Problem?

Work It Out

Maribelle has a piece of fabric with an area of 48 inches.

What are the possible lengths and widths of Maribelle's piece of fabric?

_____

_____

_____

WRITE ABOUT IT

_____

_____

What's the Problem?

Greg took a survey to find out which sport people liked the best. He asked 120 students to name their favorite sport. The results are shown on the graph.

How many students voted for each sport?

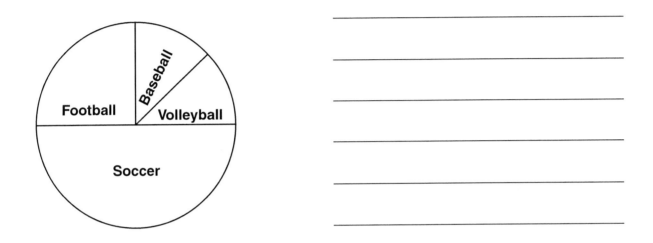

_____

_____

_____

_____

_____

_____

What's the Problem?

Marcy kept track of how students got to school. There were 100 students in her survey. Half of the students came by car. One-quarter of the students walked, and the rest rode the bus.

Make a pie chart showing Marcy's results. Label each section with the number of students represented.

What's the Problem?

Vanna picked 3 different single-digit number combinations from the choices 2, 4, 6, or 8. She did not repeat any numbers in each combination.

Which 3 number combinations could Vanna have picked?

Example: 2, 4, 6; 2, 6, 4

_____

_____

_____

_____

What's the Problem?

If two 6-sided dice are rolled, what number combinations are possible?

_____

_____

_____

_____

Which sum occurs the most often?

_____

Warm-Up 175

What's the Problem?

Count the number of buttons on 10 classmates' clothes.

Make a graph showing the results.

What is the average number of buttons worn by each classmate?

_____

Write a statement about your findings.

_____

_____

_____

Warm-Up 176

What's the Problem?

Make a graph showing the type of shoes worn by 10 classmates.

Which type of shoe is the most common?

_____

Write a statement about your findings.

_____

_____

_____

What's the Problem?

There are 10 gumdrops in a bag. There are 6 blue gumdrops, 3 red gumdrops, and 1 yellow gumdrop.

What are the chances of pulling out a blue gumdrop?

_____

What's the Problem?

Thora wrote each letter of the alphabet on its own card. She put the cards in a bag.

What are Thora's chances of pulling out a vowel?

_____

What are the chances of pulling out a consonant?

_____

Warm-Up 179

What's the Problem?

Take 1 suit of cards out of a deck of playing cards. Shuffle the cards you took out of the deck and turn over the first card. Guess whether the next card will be higher or lower. Record your guess. Turn the next card over and record the result. Then guess whether the third card will be higher or lower than the last card you turned over. Record your guess. Turn the third card over and record the result. Repeat these steps for the rest of the cards. Chart your results on a graph.

Write a sentence about your results.

Note: Cards in order from lowest to highest: A, 2, 3, 4, 5, 6, 7, 8, 9, 10, Jack, Queen, King

_____

_____

Warm-Up 180

What's the Problem?

Using the entire deck of cards, turn over the first card. Guess whether the next card will be higher or lower. Record your guess. Turn the card over and record the result. Repeat this process until 10 guesses have been made.

Chart your results on a graph.

Write a sentence about your results.

_____

_____

What's the Problem?

Sharon made this spinner.

Is it fair? Why?

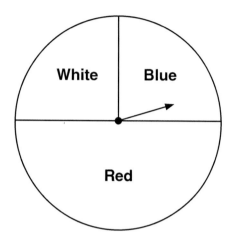

_____

_____

_____

_____

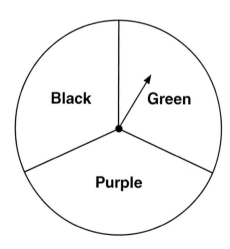

What's the Problem?

Teddy made this spinner.

If he spun it 10 times, what would it land on the most often? Why?

_____

_____

_____

_____

What's the Problem?

Jerry flipped a penny 10 times. He used tally marks to show his results.

Penny Side	Flipping Results
IN GOD WE TRUST LIBERTY 2000	☰☰☰	
UNITED STATES ONE CENT					

Make a bar graph to show Jerry's results.

Are Jerry's results reasonable? Why?

_____

_____

· ·

What's the Problem?

Darlene rolled a die 10 times. She used tally marks to show her results.

Die	·	··	·.·	::	:·:	:::
Rolling Results							☰☰	

Make a bar graph to show Darlene's results.

Are Darlene's results reasonable? Why?

_____

_____

What's the Problem?

Leslie used tally marks to keep track of the first 20 vehicles that drove by.

Based on Leslie's information, which type of vehicle would be the 21st one to drive by? Why?

Vehicle	Number That Drove By
SUV		
Motorcycle					
RV	~~				~~
Sedan			
Truck	~~|		|~~			

_____

_____

_____

_____

. . . .

What's the Problem?

Alex walked past 22 houses. He used tally marks to keep track of each house's color.

Make a pie chart using Alex's data.

When combined, which 2 house colors make up half of the pie chart?

_____

House Color	Number of Houses
Red	~~				~~
Brown				
Beige		
Green	~~|		|~~	
White		
Blue					
Yellow			

What's the Problem?

Put 5 of each coin (penny, nickel, dime, and quarter) in a bag. Without looking, pull out a coin, record the result, and put the coin back in the bag. Repeat these steps nine more times.

Make a graph to show your results.

What was the range?

_____

What was the mean?

_____

What was the mode?

_____

What's the Problem?

Phil took 5 math tests. His scores were 95%, 93%, 93%, 92%, and 94%.

What was the range?

_____

What was the median?

_____

What was the mode?

_____

What's the Problem?

Norma has 2 quarters.

If you flip both coins, what are the chances that both quarters will land on heads?

_____

What's the Problem?

Myron has 3 nickels.

If you flip all 3 coins, what are the chances that all 3 nickels will land on tails?

_____

What's the Problem?

Barbara thinks she has a 50-50, or equal chance, of rolling 2 dice with an even total. Barbara rolled the dice 10 times. She had totals of 7, 8, 10, 5, 6, 9, 7, 10, 8, and 8.

What do her results show?

_____

_____

Was Barbara's prediction correct? Why?

_____

_____

_____

- -

What's the Problem?

Matt has 3 dice. He thinks he will have a greater chance of getting an odd total than an even total when he rolls the dice. Matt rolls the dice 10 times. He has totals of 16, 10, 7, 11, 10, 14, 13, 11, 12, and 10.

What do his results show?

_____

_____

Was Matt's prediction correct? Why?

_____

_____

What's the Problem?

Judy asked people if they had a landline, cell phone, or both. Seven people had landlines. Eight people had cell phones. And 5 people had both landlines and cell phones. Judy made a Venn diagram to show her results.

What does Judy's Venn diagram look like?

· ·

What's the Problem?

Rudy asked 45 people which month they were born in. The results are in the chart.

Plot Rudy's results on a line graph.

Find the range and mode.

Month	Number of People with Birthdays
Jan.	6
Feb.	3
Mar.	1
Apr.	1
May	5
June	5
July	5
Aug.	3
Sept.	4
Oct.	1
Nov.	6
Dec.	5

What's the Problem?

Dr. McIntyre works at a busy veterinary hospital. This morning, 10 pets came in. The first 8 pets were dogs, followed by a cat, and then a potbellied pig.

Which animal is most likely to be Dr. McIntyre's next patient? Why?

_____

_____

_____

What's the Problem?

When pets are brought to the veterinary hospital, they are weighed. The first 9 pets of the day weighed 17 pounds, 29 pounds, 33 pounds, 47 pounds, 62 pounds, 1 pound, 8 pounds, 55 pounds, 62 pounds.

What is the range?

_____

What is the mode?

_____

What is the median?

_____

What's the Problem?

Mr. Simpson gives 1 pop quiz each week.

If today is Monday, what are the chances that the pop quiz will be given today?

_____

If today is Friday and no pop quiz has been given yet this week, what are the chances that the pop quiz will be given today?

_____

· ·

What's the Problem?

There are twenty students in Selena's class. One day each month, each student is line leader for the day.

If today is the first school day of the month, what are Selena's chances of being line leader?

_____

If today is the fifteenth school day of the month, what are Selena's chances of being line leader?

_____

What's the Problem?

Anthony has a 9-sided die. The die is numbered 1 through 9.

What are the chances that Anthony will roll an odd number?

_____

What are the chances that Anthony will roll an even number?

_____

What's the Problem?

Carolyn has a 12-sided die. The die is numbered 1 through 12.

What are the chances that Carolyn will roll a number greater than 6?

_____

What are the chances that Carolyn will roll an even number greater than 6?

_____

What's the Problem?

Marisa took a survey. She asked 50 people if they were left-handed or right-handed. There were 43 right-handed people and 7 left-handed people.

Make a graph showing Marisa's results.

Write a statement about the results.

_____

_____

_____

What's the Problem?

Tamika kept track of the weather for a month. There were 5 sunny days, 12 rainy days, and 13 snowy days.

Make a graph showing Tamika's results.

It is likely that the next day will be sunny? Why or why not?

_____

_____

_____

What's the Problem?

Marisol is in third grade. The morning recess is at 10:30. It is now 10:15.

What are the chances of Marisol having morning recess today? Why?

_____

_____

_____

· ·

What's the Problem?

On school nights, Nigel has a 9 o'clock bedtime. It's Wednesday night, and his favorite television program starts at 10:00 p.m.

What are Nigel's chances of being able to stay up late to watch the program? Why?

_____

_____

_____

Warm-Up
205

What's the Problem?

Jerome made a chart showing the types of hats that 100 people wore to a football game.

Write 3 questions that can be answered by using the information in Jerome's chart.

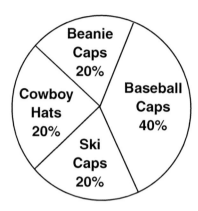

1. _____

_____

2. _____

_____

3. _____

_____

Warm-Up
206

What's the Problem?

Laurel kept track of her height over the years.

Which type of graph—pie chart, bar graph, or line graph—would best show her change in height over the years? Why?

Age	Height
3 years old	34 inches
4 years old	36 inches
5 years old	39 inches
6 years old	42 inches
7 years old	47 inches
8 years old	48 inches

_____

_____

_____

_____

_____

Warm-Up
207

What's the Problem?

Jeff wants to make a graph showing his model car collection. He has 40 cars in his collection. Ten of them are SUVs, 10 are coupes, 5 are sports cars, and 15 are racecars.

Which type of graph—line graph, pie chart, or pictograph—would best show his entire car collection? Why?

_____

_____

_____

· ·

Warm-Up
208

What's the Problem?

Matilda made a graph showing her jewelry.

Using the results below, make another graph to show Matilda's jewelry.

Which kind of graph did you make? Why?

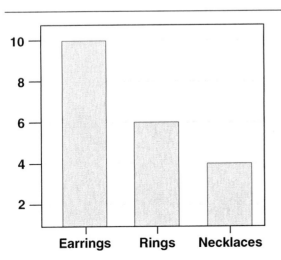

Warm-Up 209

What's the Problem?

Every Saturday, Gene goes fishing with his dad. They never catch anything other than weeds and rocks.

Is it likely that Gene will catch a fish this Saturday? Why or why not?

_____

_____

_____

Warm-Up 210

What's the Problem?

Thelma always has plans on Saturday. Sometimes she goes to the library, and other times she takes an art class.

Is it likely that Thelma will go to the library this Saturday? Why or why not?

_____

_____

_____

What's the Problem?

Work It Out

The Marshmallow Machine plops out marshmallows every time the handle is pulled. The first time, it plops out 7 marshmallows, then 13, 19, and 25 marshmallows.

How many marshmallows will plop out the tenth time the handle is pulled?

_____

WRITE ABOUT IT

_____

_____

• •

What's the Problem?

Work It Out

Phillip kept track of the turtle population at the nearby pond. He made this chart.

How many turtles will Phillip see in the fifth week?

_____

Week Number	Number of Turtles Seen
1	4
2	8
3	16
4	32
5	

WRITE ABOUT IT

_____

Algebra: logical thinking

What's the Problem?

Place the numbers 1–9 in each row and column.

Each number can appear only one time in each row and column. Also, each number can appear only one time in each 3-square by 3-square area.

Work It Out

8	3	9		4		2		
			1	3	8		4	
4						7	8	3
1	9	2	4	7	5			6
	5				3	9		4
		7		8	6			1
5			7		2	4	9	
9		4	8		1		6	
7	8	6	3		4		5	

WRITE ABOUT IT

What's the Problem?

Rachel has to put 9 numbers in the square below. No number can be used twice. The sum of each row and column must equal 42. Rachel can only use the numbers 10 through 20.

What could Rachel's arrangement look like?

Work It Out

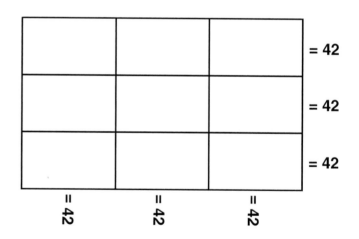

WRITE ABOUT IT

Warm-Up 215

What's the Problem?

Work It Out

Mom earned 573,319 frequent flyer miles. Dad earned 421,569 frequent flyer miles.

How many frequent flyer miles did they earn in all?

_____

WRITE ABOUT IT

_____

_____

· ·

Warm-Up 216

What's the Problem?

Work It Out

Grandma has traveled 765,863 miles. Grandpa has traveled 134,018 miles.

How many more miles has Grandma traveled?

_____

WRITE ABOUT IT

_____

Algebra: addition, subtraction

_____

What's the Problem?

Work It Out

There are 4 children in the Lopez family: Osbaldo, Maria, Fernando, and Shakira. Osbaldo is the youngest, and Maria is the oldest. Altogether, the children's ages have a sum of 34 years.

How old is each child?

_____

_____

_____

Clues
1. Maria is 12.
2. Shakira is twice as old as Osbaldo.
3. Fernando is 7.

WRITE ABOUT IT

_____

_____

What's the Problem?

Work It Out

Each year, the zookeeper weighs the animals. Today, the zookeeper is weighing the zebra, the giraffe, and the tortoise. The giraffe weighs as much as the zebra and 2 tortoises combined. The zebra weighs twice as much as the tortoise. The combined weight of all 3 animals is 3,150 pounds.

How much does each animal weigh?

_____

Note: The tortoise weighs 450 pounds.

WRITE ABOUT IT

What's the Problem?

Work It Out

Stewart ran half as many laps as Sonya. Together, they ran a total of 24 laps.

How many laps did each person run?

_____

_____

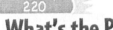

WRITE ABOUT IT

_____

_____

· ·

Warm-Up 220

What's the Problem?

Work It Out

Maurice sold magazines for a school fund-raiser. He sold the same number of fashion magazines as news magazines. He sold as many sports magazines as fashion and news magazines combined. Altogether, he sold 48 magazines.

How many of each magazine did Maurice sell?

_____

_____

WRITE ABOUT IT

_____

_____

What's the Problem?

Work It Out

Emily has 10 coins in her pocket. She has at least 1 of each coin (including half-dollar and dollar coins) and no more than 3 of each coin.

What is the least amount of money that Emily could have in her pocket?

_____

What is the greatest amount of money that Emily could have in her pocket?

_____

WRITE
ABOUT IT

_____

_____

What's the Problem?

Work It Out

Jonah has some toys in his pocket. There are 7 toys and 14 legs in all. There is an odd number of figurines (human-looking toys) in his pocket. There are the same number of 4-legged animals and balls.

How many of each toy does Jonah have in his pocket?

_____

_____

WRITE
ABOUT IT

_____

_____

What's the Problem?

Work It Out

Candy, Ryan, Elise, and Jacob are standing in a line. The 2 girls are in the middle.

How many possible arrangements are there? List them.

_____

_____

_____

_____

WRITE ABOUT IT

What's the Problem?

Work It Out

Karina collected twice as many pennies as Brandi and four times as many pennies as Bill. Altogether, they collected 700 pennies.

How many pennies did each person collect?

_____

_____

_____

WRITE ABOUT IT

What's the Problem?

Work It Out

Evan has to figure out the last number in the safe's secret combination. So far, the combination is 1 – 4 – 13 – 40 – _____.

What is the last number in the combination?

_____

What is the rule?

_____

WRITE ABOUT IT

_____

_____

What's the Problem?

Work It Out

Raquel forgot the combination to her locker. She remembered the first 3 digits. They are 40 – 32 – 24 – _____.

What is the last number in her locker combination?

_____

What is the rule?

_____

_____

WRITE ABOUT IT

_____

What's the Problem?

All of the parentheses fell out of Lee's math book.

Where should the parentheses go to make the math problem correct?

Work It Out

2 x 4 + 6 = 20

What's the Problem?

Annie wrote the math problem down but forgot to add the parentheses.

Where should the parentheses go to make the math problem correct?

Work It Out

6 x 2 + 4 = 36

WRITE ABOUT IT

What's the Problem?

The Number Company's number machine stopped working.

What are the missing numbers in the pattern? Add them to the chart.

What is the rule?

_____

_____

> WRITE ABOUT IT

Work It Out

In	Out
1	3
3	9
5	15
7	
9	
11	

· ·

What's the Problem?

Victoria used a stick to write this pattern in the dirt.

What should the next 3 numbers in the pattern be?

_____

What is the rule?

_____

_____

> WRITE ABOUT IT

Work It Out

100, 10, 90, 20,_____, _____, _____

What's the Problem?

Bernie has the numbers 31, 13, and 18.

How can the numbers be arranged to make a true math problem?

Work It Out

_____ + _____ = _____

> WRITE
> ABOUT IT

_____

_____

• •

What's the Problem?

Beatrix has the numbers 13, 28, and 41.

How can the numbers be arranged to make a true math problem?

Work It Out

_____ − _____ = _____

> WRITE
> ABOUT IT

_____

_____

What's the Problem?

Work It Out

Kitty has a book bag. Her book bag can hold 3 books and up to ten pounds.

Which books could Kitty have in her book bag? List one combination.

Item	Weight
Library book	2 pounds
Math book	3 pounds
Reading book	4 pounds
History book	5 pounds
Science book	6 pounds
Notebook	1 pound
Spelling book	3 pounds
Dictionary	5 pounds

_____

_____

_____

WRITE ABOUT IT

Warm-Up 234

What's the Problem?

Work It Out

Taylor stacked blocks into 3 different stacks. Each stack is a different height. He has 23 blocks in all.

What is one way that Taylor could stack the blocks?

_____

_____

_____

WRITE ABOUT IT

Warm-Up 235

What's the Problem?

Work It Out

Angie is writing an equation to go with a word problem. The word problem reads, "Giovanni had 27 marbles. He lost some of them during a tournament. He has 19 left."

What should Angie's equation look like?

_____

Solve the equation.

_____

WRITE ABOUT IT

_____

_____

• •

Warm-Up 236

What's the Problem?

Work It Out

Derek is writing an equation to go with a word problem. The word problem reads, "There are 500 students in the school. Every day, they either eat hot lunches or cold lunches. Two hundred seventeen kids eat cold lunches every day. How many students each hot lunches?"

What should Derek's equation look like?

_____

Solve the equation.

_____

WRITE ABOUT IT

_____

What's the Problem?

Work It Out

Tilly needs to find the prime numbers between 1 and 20.

Besides 2 and 3, what are the other prime numbers?

_____

_____

_____

WRITE
ABOUT IT

_____

_____

- -

Warm-Up
238

What's the Problem?

Work It Out

Rocky thinks 51 is a prime number.

Is he correct? Why?

_____

_____

_____

WRITE
ABOUT IT

_____

What's the Problem?

Work It Out

Bobby was given this equation in math class: $4x = 16$.

How should Bobby solve this problem?

_____

_____

_____

WRITE ABOUT IT

- -

Warm-Up 240

What's the Problem?

Work It Out

Margaret copied the problem from the board. She wrote in her notebook $3x + 3 = 18$.

How much is x worth?

_____

WRITE ABOUT IT

Warm-Up 241

What's the Problem?

Work It Out

Benita needs to write the following word problem as an equation. "Wiley made 9 shirts. He used a total of 63 buttons in all. How many buttons were on each shirt?"

What should the problem look like?

_____

Solve the equation.

_____

WRITE ABOUT IT

_____

. . . .

Warm-Up 242

What's the Problem?

Work It Out

Buzz read the following word problem and then wrote it as an equation. "A bus can hold 78 children if they sit 3 to a seat. How many seats are on the bus?"

What equation did Buzz write?

_____

Solve the equation.

_____

WRITE ABOUT IT

What's the Problem?

Mom bought twice as many cans of peaches as pears. She bought 12 cans in all.

How many cans of each fruit did Mom buy?

_____

_____

_____

WRITE ABOUT IT

Work It Out

_____

_____

- -

What's the Problem?

Dad has three times as many nickels as pennies. He has 20 coins in all.

How many of each coin does Dad have?

_____

_____

WRITE ABOUT IT

Work It Out

_____

_____

_____

Warm-Up 245

What's the Problem?

Sally wrote the number pattern on a long strip of paper.

What should the next 3 numbers be?

_____

What is the rule?

_____

_____

WRITE ABOUT IT

Work It Out

1, 4, 16, 64, _____ , _____ , _____

Warm-Up 246

What's the Problem?

As Wally walked past each office building, he wrote down its number.

What numbers will the next 3 businesses have?

_____

What is the rule?

_____

_____

WRITE ABOUT IT

Work It Out

12000, 6000, 3000, _____ , _____ , _____

Warm-Up 247

What's the Problem?

Minerva needs to write the missing symbols to make the math problem correct.

What are the symbols?

Work It Out

(23 _____ 23) _____ 11 = 57

WRITE ABOUT IT

_____

_____

Warm-Up 248

What's the Problem?

Ashton needs to write the missing symbols to make the math problem correct.

What are the symbols?

Work It Out

4 _____ (10 _____ 10) = 400

WRITE ABOUT IT

_____

_____

What's the Problem?

Work It Out

Bess needs to write the following problem as an equation. "Micah bought 6 pairs of shoes for a total of 12 shoes in all." Bess needs to use 1 variable in the equation.

What is the equation?

_____

Solve the equation.

_____

WRITE ABOUT IT

What's the Problem?

Work It Out

Robert needs to write the following problem as an equation. "Chelsea counted 9 sets of triplets for 27 kids in all." Robert needs to use 1 variable in the equation.

What is the equation?

_____

Solve the equation.

_____

WRITE ABOUT IT

Warm-Up 1

Work It Out

●●□☼❀♡♥●●❀□☼♡♥❀●●●☼□❀♥☼●●☼❀

There are 7 beads (positions 1, 2, 8, 9, 16, 17, 23).

There are 3 squares (positions 3, 11, 19).

There are 3 suns (positions 4, 13, 22).

There are 5 flowers (positions 5, 10, 15, 20, 25).

There are 4 stars (positions 6, 12, 18, 24).

There are 3 hearts (positions 7, 14, 21).

Problem Solved

Georgia used 7 beads. Georgia used 18 charms.

Warm-Up 2

Work It Out

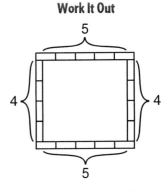

$$5 + 4 + 5 + 4 = 18$$

Problem Solved

Ben needs 18 bricks to surround a 5-foot by 5-foot area.

Warm-Up 3

Work It Out

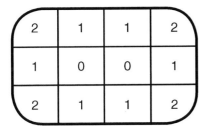

Problem Solved

Two brownies have no crispy edges. Six brownies have 1 crispy edge. Four brownies have 2 crispy edges.

Warm-Up 4

Work It Out

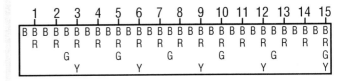

Problem Solved

Jen will use 30 blue nails, 15 red nails, 6 green nails, and 5 yellow nails. At 15 inches, all 4 nail colors will be used.

Warm-Up 5

Work It Out

10"	10"	10"	10"	2"
10"	10"	10"	10"	2"
10"	10"	10"	10"	2"
6"	6"	6"	6"	2"

Problem Solved

Kasey can cut twelve 10-inch squares.

Warm-Up 6

Work It Out

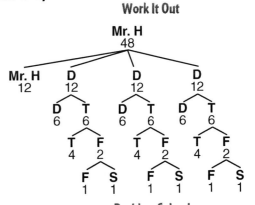

Problem Solved

Mr. Harmony ended up with 12 pieces. Each drummer had 6 pieces. Each tuba player had 4 pieces. Each flute and saxophone player had 1 piece.

Warm-Up 7

Work It Out

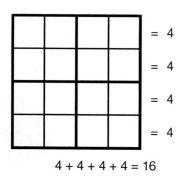

				= 4
				= 4
				= 4
				= 4

4 + 4 + 4 + 4 = 16

Problem Solved

There are 16 squares in all.

Warm-Up 8

Work It Out

8 legs:

A(1st) B*(2nd)* C*(3rd)* D*(4th)* E*(5th)* F*(6th)* G*(7th)* H*(8th)*
A shakes hands with B, C, D, E, F, G, and H.
B shakes hands with C, D, E, F, G, and H.
C shakes hands with D, E, F, G, and H.
D shakes hands with E, F, G, and H.
E shakes hands with F, G, and H.
F shakes hands with G and H.
G shakes hands with H.

7 + 6 + 5 + 4 + 3 + 2 + 1 = 28

Problem Solved

Ollie can shake hands with himself 28 times.

Warm-Up 9

Work It Out

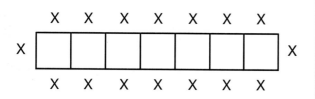

Problem Solved

Seven tables will be needed.

Warm-Up 10

Work It Out

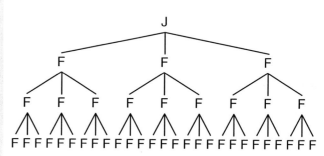

1 + 3 + 9 + 27 = 40

Problem Solved

Forty people know the secret.

Warm-Up 11

Work It Out

Item	Amount Used	Amount Unused
C. Chips	50	50
C. Candies	25	75
Walnuts	40	60

Problem Solved

Clint uses 50 chocolate chips, 25 chocolate candies, and 40 walnuts. There are 50 chocolate chips, 75 chocolate candies, and 60 walnuts left.

Warm-Up 12

Work It Out

	Parents	Babies & Spouses	B & S Babies		
Members of the Rabbit Family	Mr. R Mrs. R	R + R	B	B	B
			B	B	B
		R + R	B	B	B
			B	B	B
		R + R	B	B	B
			B	B	B
		R + R	B	B	B
			B	B	B
		R + R	B	B	B
			B	B	B
		R + R	B	B	B
			B	B	B
Total Number of Rabbits	2	12	36		

2 + 12 + 36 = 50

Problem Solved

There are 50 rabbits in the Rabbit family.

ANSWER KEY *(cont.)*

Warm-Up 13

Work It Out

Style	Color	Design
Knee-High	White	Dog
		Cat
	Red	Dog
		Cat
Ankle-High	White	Dog
		Cat
	Red	Dog
		Cat

Problem Solved

There are eight possible sock combinations.

Warm-Up 14

Work It Out

Sample answer:

	Number of Teeth	Amount Paid	Number of Teeth	Amount Paid	Number of Teeth	Amount Paid
Molars	1	$2.50	2	$5.00	4	$10.00
Incisors	1	$1.50	2	$3.00	2	$3.00
Total	2	$4.00	4	$8.00	6	$13.00

Problem Solved

Jeffrey has lost 4 molars and 2 incisors.

Warm-Up 15

Work It Out

Rate	Su	M	T	W	Th	F	S
$0.30		10	10	10	10	10	10
$0.60	10						
Total	$6.00	$3.00	$3.00	$3.00	$3.00	$3.00	$3.00

$6.00 + $3.00 + $3.00 + $3.00 + $3.00 + $3.00 + $3.00 = $24.00

Problem Solved

Taylor earns $24.00 each week.

Warm-Up 16

Work It Out

	2-Digit Numbers		3-Digit Numbers			4-Digit Numbers		
	36	81	368	681	861	3,681	6,318	8,163
	38	13	386	618	816	3,618	6,381	8,136
	31	16	361	631	136	3,816	6,138	1,368
	63	18	316	613	163	3,861	6,183	1,386
	68		381	836	138	3,186	8,361	1,863
	61		318	863	183	3,168	8,316	1,836
	83		638	831	168	6,813	8,631	1,683
	86		683	813	186	6,831	8,613	1,638
Total	12		24			24		

12 + 24 + 24 = 60

Problem Solved

Sixty different numbers can be made.

Warm-Up 17

Work It Out

Sample answers:

H-D	Q	D	N	Total Coins
4	0	0	0	4
3	2	0	0	5
3	1	1	5	10
3	0	3	4	10
2	4	0	0	6
2	3	2	1	8
2	3	1	3	9
1	6	0	0	7
1	5	2	1	9
1	4	5	0	10

Problem Solved

Check to make sure the student listed the ways $2.00 can be made using 10 or fewer coins.

Warm-Up 18

Work It Out

$24.00	$13.00	$8.00	= $45.00
$12.00	$10.00	$23.00	= $45.00
$9.00	$22.00	$14.00	= $45.00

= $45.00   = $45.00   = $45.00

Problem Solved

Check to make sure the student's rows and columns each equal $45.00.

Warm-Up 19

Work It Out

Sample answer:

Pants	Shirts
Blue	Red
	Orange
	Yellow
Green	Red
	Orange
	Yellow
Purple	Red
	Orange
	Yellow

Problem Solved

Cynthia can make 9 different outfits.

Warm-Up 20

Work It Out

Sample answer:

Person	Weight in Pounds				
Jeb	5	20	40	35	34
Corinne	10	40	80	70	68
Ben	20	80	160	140	136
Total Pounds	35	140	280	245	238

Problem Solved

Jeb weighs 34 pounds, Corinne weighs 68 pounds, and Ben weighs 136 pounds.

Warm-Up 21

Work It Out

Students can use counters to determine how many people are on the bus.

$$10 + 10 - 5 + 10 - 9 + 4 = 20$$

Problem Solved

There are 20 people on the bus.

Warm-Up 22

Work It Out

Students can use grapes or counters to determine the amount of grapes each person will receive.

$$\begin{array}{r} 9 \\ 9 \\ 9 \\ +9 \\ \hline 36 \end{array}$$

9 → Lindsey
9 → #1
9 → #2
+9 → #3

Problem Solved

Each person will receive 9 grapes.

Warm-Up 23

Work It Out

Students can use counters or craft sticks to determine which is more.

64

$\frac{1}{2}$ of 64 = 32

$\frac{1}{4}$ of 32 = 8

27

$\frac{1}{3}$ of 27 = 9

Problem Solved

One-third of 27 is more than $\frac{1}{4}$ of $\frac{1}{2}$ of 64.

Warm-Up 24

Work It Out

Students can use two different colors of counters to determine how many students are on each team.

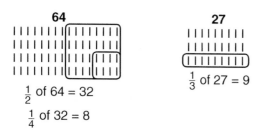

20 Students

Red ←→ Blue

Red			Blue
○○○○○○○○○○	10	10	○○○○○○○○○○
○○○○○	−5	+5	○○○○○
○○○○	+4	−4	○○○○
○○○○○○	−6	+6	○○○○○○
○○○○○○○○○	+9	−9	○○○○○○○○○
	12	8	

Problem Solved

There are 12 students on the Red team and 8 students on the Blue team.

Warm-Up 25

Work It Out

Students can use pattern block triangles to determine what shapes can be made.

Sample answers:

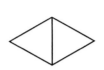 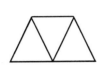 

Problem Solved

Rhombi, trapezoids, and hexagons can all be made using only pattern block triangles.

Warm-Up 26

Work It Out

Students can stack nickels and determine their quantity and value.

14 nickels = 1 inch

14 nickels x 12 inches = 168 nickels

168 nickels x $0.05 = $8.40

Problem Solved

There are 168 nickels in a 1-foot stack. They are worth $8.40.

Warm-Up 27

Work It Out

Students can stack nickels and dimes and determine their value.

14 nickels = 1 inch

11 dimes = $\frac{1}{2}$ inch

Eleven dimes are worth $1.10 and 14 nickels are worth $0.70.

Problem Solved

The $\frac{1}{2}$-inch stack of dimes is worth more than the 1-inch stack of nickels.

Warm-Up 28

Work It Out

Students can use pencil boxes and pencils to determine the age of Ricky's mom.

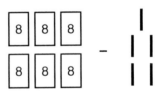

8 candles in a box x 6 boxes = 48 candles
48 candles – 5 leftover candles = 43

Problem Solved

Ricky's mom is 43 years old.

Warm-Up 29

Work It Out

Students can use toy cars to determine how many parent drivers are needed.

Twenty-nine students divided by 4 per car = 7 cars + 1 student leftover.

The remaining student will need a parent to drive.

Problem Solved

Eight parent drivers are needed.

Warm-Up 30

Work It Out

Check to make sure the student used crayons to determine the perimeter of his or her desk.

Problem Solved

Answers will vary.

Warm-Up 31

Work It Out

Students can make an educated guess, check it for accuracy, and continue making guesses until reaching the correct answer.

Problem Solved

Four students voted for the snake, 6 students voted for the hamster, and 12 students voted for the bird.

Warm-Up 32

Work It Out

Students can make an educated guess, check it for accuracy, and continue making guesses until reaching the correct answer.

Problem Solved

There are 3 possible window sizes: 1 foot by 5 feet, 2 feet by 4 feet, and 3 feet by 3 feet.

Warm-Up 33

Work It Out

Students can make an educated guess, check it for accuracy, and continue making guesses until reaching the correct answer.

Sample answer:

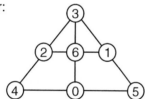

Problem Solved

Check to make sure that all the student's lines have a sum of 9.

Warm-Up 34

Work It Out

Students can make an educated guess, check it for accuracy, and continue making guesses until reaching the correct answer.

Sample answer:

16	14	21	= 51
15	19	17	= 51
20	18	13	= 51
= 51	= 51	= 51	

Problem Solved

Check to make sure the student's rows and columns each equal 51.

Warm-Up 35

Work It Out

Students can make an educated guess, check it for accuracy, and continue making guesses until reaching the correct answer.

Sample answer:

1 Ticket for $5.00	1	$5.00	3	$15.00	1	$5.00
Set of 2 Tickets for $7.00	1	$7.00	2	$14.00	5	$35.00
Set of 3 Tickets for $10.00	1	$10.00	2	$20.00	3	$30.00
Total		$22.00		$49.00		$70.00

Problem Solved

Jack sold 1 ticket for $5.00, five sets of 2 tickets for $7.00 each, and three sets of 3 tickets for $10.00 each.

Warm-Up 36

Work It Out

Students can make an educated guess, check it for accuracy, and continue making guesses until reaching the correct answer.

Sample answer:

Sons	2	4	6	5
Daughters	0	2	4	3
Total	2	6	10	8

Problem Solved

Mr. Souza has 5 sons and 3 daughters.

Warm-Up 37

Work It Out

Students can make an educated guess, check it for accuracy, and continue making guesses until reaching the correct answer.

Sample answer:

Raven's Pockets	4	8	12
Sayeed's Pockets	2	4	6
Nuha's Pockets	1	2	3
Total	7	14	21

Problem Solved

Raven has 12 pockets, Sayeed has 6 pockets, and Nuha has 3 pockets.

Warm-Up 38

Work It Out

Students can make an educated guess, check it for accuracy, and continue making guesses until reaching the correct answer.

Sample answer:

Girls (5 buttons)	9 45 buttons	9 45 buttons
Boys (3 buttons)	10 30 buttons	11 33 buttons
Total Buttons	75 buttons	78 buttons

Problem Solved

There are 9 girls and 11 boys in Ms. McRae's class.

Warm-Up 39

Work It Out

Students can make an educated guess, check it for accuracy, and continue making guesses until reaching the correct answer.

Sample answer:

18-cent Stamps	4	$0.72	6	$1.08
33-cent Stamps	7	$2.31	4	$1.32
Total Postage		$3.03		$2.40

Problem Solved

Yes, Sidney can use six 18-cent stamps and four 33-cent stamps.

Warm-Up 40

Work It Out

Students can make an educated guess, check it for accuracy, and continue making guesses until reaching the correct answer.

Problem Solved

The short cylinder holds more counters than the tall cylinder.

Warm-Up 41

Work It Out

1 day = 1 can
2 days = 4 cans   ⟩ + 3
3 days = 8 cans   ⟩ + 4
4 days = 13 cans   ⟩ + 5
5 days = 19 cans   ⟩ + 6

6 days = 26 cans   ⟩ +7
7 days = 34 cans   ⟩ +8
8 days = 43 cans   ⟩ +9
9 days = 53 cans   ⟩ +10
10 days = 64 cans   ⟩ +11

Problem Solved

Thomas will collect 64 cans on the tenth day.

Warm-Up 42

Work It Out

In		Out
10	(x 3)	30
8	(x 3)	24
14	(x 3)	42

Problem Solved

The rule is to multiply by 3.

Warm-Up 43

Work It Out

1	2	3	4	5	6	7	8	9	10
11	12	13	14	15	16	17	(18)	(19)	20
21	22	23	24	25	26	(27)	(28)	29	30
31	32	33	34	35	(36)	(37)	38	39	40
41	42	43	44	(45)	(46)	47	48	49	50
51	52	53	(54)	(55)	56	57	58	59	60
61	62	(63)	(64)	65	66	67	68	69	70
71	(72)	(73)	74	75	76	77	78	79	80
(81)	(82)	83	84	85	86	87	88	89	(90)
(91)	92	93	94	95	96	97	98	99	100

Problem Solved

Nine and ten are the most common sums.

Warm-Up 44

Work It Out

Day	Sheep	Mice	Pigs	Goats	Horses	Cows	Chickens	Roosters	Cats	Donkeys
1	1									
2	1	2								
3	1	2	3							
4	1	2	3	4						
5	1	2	3	4	5					
6	1	2	3	4	5	6				
7	1	2	3	4	5	6	7			
8	1	2	3	4	5	6	7	8		
9	1	2	3	4	5	6	7	8	9	
10	1	2	3	4	5	6	7	8	9	10
Total Animals	10	18	24	28	30	30	28	24	18	10

Problem Solved

Tony will receive 10 sheep, 18 mice, 24 pigs, 28 goats, 30 horses, 30 cows, 28 chickens, 24 roosters, 18 cats, and 10 donkeys. There will be 30 horses and 30 cows.

Warm-Up 45

Work It Out

Sunday   = 1
    } +1
Monday   = 2
    } +2
Tuesday   = 4
    } +3
Wednesday = 7
    } +4
Thursday   = 11
    } +5
Friday   = 16
    } +6
Saturday   = 22

Problem Solved

Lettie will do 11 chin-ups on Thursday, 16 chin-ups on Friday, and 22 chin-ups on Saturday.

Warm-Up 46

Work It Out

Holes	3	6	9	12	15	18	21	24	27	30	33	36
Seconds	5	10	15	20	25	30	35	40	45	50	55	60

Problem Solved

The machine will punch 36 holes in 1 minute.

Warm-Up 47

Work It Out

100
   } −12
88
   } +3
91
   } −12
79

82
   } +3
70
   } −12
73
   } +3
61

64
   } +3
52
   } −12
55
   } +3
43

Problem Solved

The next 3 numbers are 52, 55, and 43. The pattern will never reach 0.

Warm-Up 48

Work It Out

American Money	$1.00	$2.00	$3.00	$4.00	$5.00	$6.00	$7.00	$8.00	$9.00	$10.00
Canadian Money	$1.05	$2.10	$3.15	$4.20	$5.25	$6.30	$7.35	$8.40	$9.45	$10.50

Problem Solved

Ten dollars in American money is worth $10.50 in Canadian money.

Warm-Up 49

Work It Out

Day 1 = 100
   } +125
Day 2 = 225
   } +150
Day 3 = 375
   } +175
Day 4 = 550

Day 5 = 750
   } +200
Day 6 = 975
   } +225
Day 7 = 1,225
   } +250

Problem Solved

The elephant will eat 1,225 peanuts on day seven.

Warm-Up 50

Work It Out

Number of Students	1	2	3	4	5	6
Number of Markers	4	8	12	16	20	24

Problem Solved

Six students would share 24 markers.

ANSWER KEY (cont.)

Warm-Up 51
Arlo makes $4.80. The average selling price for the muffins is $0.20.

Warm-Up 52
Martha will earn $2.20.

Warm-Up 53
There are 285 doors and windows in all.

Warm-Up 54
Mr. Newcastle needed 270 hinges.

Warm-Up 55
Sample problems:
3 + 3 + 3 = 9
33 + 3 = 36
33 − 3 = 30
(3 − 3) + 3 = 3

Warm-Up 56
Sample problems:
(5 x 4) x 0 = 0
(3 − 2) + 0 = 1
(6 ÷ 2) − 1 = 2
(6 + 4) − 7 = 3
(9 ÷ 3) + 1 = 4
(2 x 1) + 3 = 5
(5 + 0) + 1 = 6
(3 x 4) −5 = 7
(8 ÷ 4) + 6 = 8
(2 x 4) + 1 = 9
(9 + 2) − 1 = 10

Warm-Up 57
There are 125 red gumballs, 100 blue gumballs, 175 yellow gumballs, and 100 green gumballs.

Warm-Up 58
Maggie has 50 gumballs, Scott has 10 gumballs, Bailey has 20 gumballs, Spencer has 10 gumballs, and Sally has 10 gumballs.

Warm-Up 59
I would rather be paid $1.75 to start. At $5 each week, I would earn $20.00. If I were paid $1.75 per week and it doubled each week, I would earn $26.25.

Warm-Up 60
Jim will earn $15.36 for the tenth cup. He will earn a total of $30.69.

Warm-Up 61
Antonio typed an average of 18 wpm.

Warm-Up 62
Antonio typed 16 wpm. No, his speed decreased.

Warm-Up 63
Answers will vary.

Warm-Up 64
Answers will vary.

Warm-Up 65
Garth will earn $3.05 for numbering a 100-page book.

Warm-Up 66
Betty will write the digit 1, 21 times.

Warm-Up 67
Ben and Keith will both touch the ball 3 times. Pat will touch the ball 5 times.

Warm-Up 68
Chris will toss the Frisbee 5 times. Chuck will toss the Frisbee 3 times. Alicia will toss the Frisbee 2 times.

Warm-Up 69
Connie put $40.00 in her college savings account.

Warm-Up 70
There were 25 walnuts (25%) and 25 raisins (25%) in the bag.

Warm-Up 71
Answers will vary. Check to make sure the student's answer is $35.00 or less.

Warm-Up 72
Nigel's cell phone bill was $10.30.

Warm-Up 73
Sample answers:
number word
(*seven hundred eighty-nine*)
numbers and words
(7 *hundreds* 8 *tens* 9 *ones*)
numbers (700 + 80 + 9)
place value blocks
(7 hundred flats, 8 ten rods, 9 ones)

Warm-Up 74
Sample answers:
number word (*one thousand two hundred sixty-three*)
numbers and words (1 *thousand* 2 *hundreds* 6 *tens* 3 *ones*)
numbers (1,000 + 200 + 60 + 3)
place value blocks (1 cube, 2 hundred flats, 6 ten rods, 3 ones)

Warm-Up 75
Billy will need to buy 4 bags of hot-dog buns for a total of 40 buns. He will need to buy 5 packs of hot dogs for a total of 40 hot dogs.

Warm-Up 76
Wilma will need to buy 3 bags of hamburger buns and 6 pounds of beef.

Warm-Up 77
Amy has $33.00 in her savings account.

Warm-Up 78
It will take Ross 45 weeks to save enough money to buy the scooter.

Warm-Up 79
Lawrence has 136 pages left to read.

Warm-Up 80
The children need 255 carrots in all.

Warm-Up 81
There are 3,933 adults (and 1,311 children) living in the two small towns.

Warm-Up 82

There are 1,000 adults; 250 newborns; and 1,250 children and teenagers in Sweet Water Valley.

Warm-Up 83

Anissa has 54 books. Together, the 2 sisters have 72 books.

Warm-Up 84

The farmer needs 1,578 acres of land.

Warm-Up 85

Jamie has $6.25 in quarters.

Warm-Up 86

No, Nancy does not have enough money to pay for the items. She needs $7.00 more.

Warm-Up 87

In Brianna's Scout Troop, 18 kids are 9 years old and 12 kids are 8 years old.

Warm-Up 88

Harris will pay $44.80 for the new ice skates.

Warm-Up 89

There were 16 pieces of candy in the bag. Bill ate 8 pieces of candy on Monday, 4 pieces of candy on Tuesday, and 2 pieces of candy on Wednesday. He has 2 candies left.

Warm-Up 90

The third girl ate $\frac{5}{12}$ of the pizza.

Warm-Up 91

The pawn can get to the other side of the board using 5 moves. The knight can get to the other side of the board using 4 moves. The knight uses fewer moves.

Warm-Up 92

The bishop can get to the other side of the board using 2 moves. The king can get to the other side of the board using 7 moves. The bishop uses fewer moves.

Warm-Up 93

It will take 15 toothpicks to make 7 triangles.

Warm-Up 94

It will take 12 toothpicks to make 4 squares.

Warm-Up 95

The perimeter of the triangle is 27 cm.

Warm-Up 96

The perimeter of the square is 32 cm.

Warm-Up 97

The perimeter of the rectangle is 20 inches.

Warm-Up 98

The perimeter of the trapezoid is 21 inches.

Warm-Up 99

The total area is 6 square units. The perimeter is 14 units.

Warm-Up 100

The shape is a rectangle. The perimeter will vary.

Warm-Up 101

The area of the grid is 32 square units.

Warm-Up 102

The area of the grid is 64 square units.

Warm-Up 103

Sample answers:

The numbers 0, 1, 3, and 8 have horizontal lines of symmetry. The numbers 0 and 8 also have vertical lines of symmetry.

Warm-Up 104

The letters A, H, I, M, O, T, U, V, W, X, and Y have vertical lines of symmetry. The letters B, C, D, E, H, I, K, O, and X have horizontal lines of symmetry.

Warm-Up 105

Sample answers:

square, rectangle, trapezoid, rhombus, parallelogram

Warm-Up 106

Sample answers:

pentagon, hexagon, octagon, decagon

Warm-Up 107

Answers will vary.

Warm-Up 108

Answers will vary.

Warm-Up 109

triangles: 3; 4

trapezoids: 2; 1 and 3; 4 and 5; 2 and 5

rhombus: 5; 1

hexagon: 1, 2, and 3

Warm-Up 110

triangles: 2; 3; 4; 7; 8; 9

trapezoid: 1, 2, 3, 4, 5; 6, 7, 8, 9, 10; 1, 2, 3; 3, 4, 5; 6, 7, 8; 8, 9, 10

rhombus: 1 and 2; 3 and 8; 4 and 5; 6 and 7; 9 and 10

hexagon: 1–10; 1, 2, 3, 6, 7, 8; 3, 4, 5, 8, 9, 10

Warm-Up 111

Answers will vary.

Warm-Up 112

Answers will vary.

Warm-Up 113

Sample answers:

number of sides, number of corners, curved edges, straight edges

Warm-Up 114

Sample answers:

number of sides, number of corners

Warm-Up 115

Top	checkers
	cards
	marbles
	blocks
	coloring books
Bottom	chess set

Warm-Up 116
1st—red
2nd—orange
3rd—yellow
4th—green
5th—blue
6th—purple

Warm-Up 117
Jeremy made a triangle, a
rhombus, and a trapezoid.

Warm-Up 118
Renee drew 1 line to make 2
squares. Then she drew a diagonal
line on 1 square to make 2
triangles.

Warm-Up 119
She can make a rectangular
pyramid. It will have 5 corners.

Warm-Up 120
She can make a triangular prism.
It will have 6 corners.

Warm-Up 121
4 different ways:

Warm-Up 122
1 way:

Warm-Up 123
Sample answers:
hexagon, parallelogram

Warm-Up 124
Sample answers:
hexagon, parallelogram

Warm-Up 125
7 triangles:
2 large triangles; 2 small
triangles; 1 medium triangle, 2
small triangles, 1 square, and 1
parallelogram; 2 small triangles
and 1 square; 2 small triangles and
1 parallelogram;1 large triangle,
2 small triangles, and 1 square;
1 large triangle, 2 small triangles,
and 1 parallelogram

Warm-Up 126
5 squares:
all 7 shapes; 2 large triangles;1
large triangle, 2 small triangles,
1 parallelogram; 1 large triangle,
1 square, and 2 small triangles; 2
small triangles

Warm-Up 127
He made a square. The perimeter
is 16.

Warm-Up 128
She made a rectangle. Perimeters
will vary.

Warm-Up 129

 or

Warm-Up 130

Warm-Up 131
The field trip is 13 hours and 30
minutes long.

Warm-Up 132
Yes, they beat the school record.
The relay team finished the race
in 252 seconds or 4 minutes and
12 seconds. That is less than 5
minutes.

Warm-Up 133
The temperature is 86°F. Julia
does not need a heavy jacket.

Warm-Up 134
The average temperature was 65°F.

Warm-Up 135
It takes 11 weeks and 3 days for
the plant to be ready to harvest.

Warm-Up 136
Johanna will have 5 birthdays
(2004, 2008, 2012, 2016, 2020).

Warm-Up 137
Jimmy ran 2.5 miles in all.

Warm-Up 138
Helen rode her bike for an average
of 13.33 miles per day.

Warm-Up 139
Recess will be over at 11:10 a.m.

Warm-Up 140
The program began at 7:45 p.m.

Warm-Up 141
Zach is 8 inches taller than Barry.

Warm-Up 142
No, Martha does not have enough
material. The material she has is 2
feet by 4 feet.

Warm-Up 143
Six yards would be 216 inches.

Warm-Up 144
The football field is 300 feet, or
3,600 inches, long.

Warm-Up 145
There are 10,000 meters in 10
kilometers.

Warm-Up 146
There are 30.48 centimeters in 1 foot.

Warm-Up 147
There are 1,440 minutes in 1 day.
There are 86,400 seconds in 1 day.

Warm-Up 148
There are 1,095 days in 3 years.

Warm-Up 149
There are 96 buns in 12 pounds.

Warm-Up 150
Eight stones weigh 112 pounds.

Warm-Up 151
There are 14 more days until
Sage's birthday.

Warm-Up 152
There are 242 or 243 more days
until summer vacation.

Warm-Up 153
David was born at 12:09 p.m.

Warm-Up 154
Jane goes to school for 1,080
hours.

Warm-Up 155
It took Jordan 8 hours and 49
minutes.

Warm-Up 156
Beverly starts her homework at
5:15 p.m.

Warm-Up 157

Kari swam for 1 hour and 48 minutes in all.

Warm-Up 158

Jason read for 1 hour and 19 minutes in all.

Warm-Up 159

People should drink 4 pints or 2 quarts of water each day.

Warm-Up 160

There are 128 ounces in 1 gallon of milk.

Warm-Up 161

It will take Ellen 7 weeks and 1 day to visit all 50 states.

Warm-Up 162

The Plymale family will be gone for 38 days.

Warm-Up 163

Allison has 4 boards: one 12-inch board, one 6-inch board, and two 3-inch boards.

Warm-Up 164

Brady's room is 4 yards by 5 yards.

Warm-Up 165

The fence is 21.8 yards long.

Warm-Up 166

Darby is 160.02 centimeters tall.

Warm-Up 167

Quita's box is 512 cubic inches.

Warm-Up 168

Hubert's box is 60 cubic inches.

Warm-Up 169

Possible window sizes:

1 foot x 24 feet

2 feet x 12 feet

3 feet x 8 feet

4 feet x 6 feet

Warm-Up 170

Possible fabric sizes:

1 inch x 48 inches

2 inches x 24 inches

3 inches x 16 inches

4 inches x 12 inches

6 inches x 8 inches

Warm-Up 171

Sixty people voted for soccer. Thirty people voted for football. Fifteen people voted for baseball. Fifteen people voted for volleyball.

Warm-Up 172

Check to make sure the student made a pie chart reflecting the following results: car—$\frac{1}{2}$ or 50%, walk—$\frac{1}{4}$ or 25%, bus—$\frac{1}{4}$ or 25%.

Warm-Up 173

Vanna has 24 choices:

2, 4, 6	4, 6, 2	6, 8, 2
2, 4, 8	4, 6, 8	6, 8, 4
2, 6, 4	4, 8, 2	8, 2, 4
2, 6, 8	4, 8, 6	8, 2, 6
2, 8, 4	6, 2, 4	8, 4, 2
2, 8, 6	6, 2, 8	8, 4, 6
4, 2, 6	6, 4, 2	8, 6, 2
4, 2, 8	6, 4, 8	8, 6, 4

Warm-Up 174

Possible number combinations:

1-1	2-4	4-1	5-4
1-2	2-5	4-2	5-5
1-3	2-6	4-3	5-6
1-4	3-1	4-4	6-1
1-5	3-2	4-5	6-2
1-6	3-3	4-6	6-3
2-1	3-4	5-1	6-4
2-2	3-5	5-2	6-5
2-3	3-6	5-3	6-6

The most common sum is 7.

Warm-Up 175

Check to make sure the student made an appropriate graph.

Answers will vary.

Warm-Up 176

Check to make sure the student made an appropriate graph.

Answers will vary.

Warm-Up 177

The chances of pulling out a blue gumdrop are 6 out of 10 or 3 out of 5.

Warm-Up 178

The chances of pulling out a vowel are 5 out of 26.

The chances of pulling out a consonant are 21 out of 26.

Warm-Up 179

Check to make sure the student made an appropriate graph.

Answers will vary.

Warm-Up 180

Check to make sure the student made an appropriate graph.

Answers will vary.

Warm-Up 181

No, it is not fair. It is more likely to land on red because $\frac{1}{2}$ of the spinner is red.

Warm-Up 182

The spinner has an equal chance of landing on black, green, or purple because the colors are divided equally.

Warm-Up 183

Check to make sure the student made a bar graph.

Yes, Jerry's results are reasonable. There is an equal chance of landing on heads or tails. His results of 6 heads and 4 tails is close to what was expected.

Warm-Up 184

Check to make sure the student made a bar graph.

No, Darlene's results are not reasonable. You would expect there to be only 1 or 2 of each number rolled. One number was never rolled, and 1 number was rolled 5 times.

Warm-Up 185

A truck would most likely drive by next, as it was the most common vehicle that Leslie saw.

Warm-Up 186

Check to make sure the student made a pie chart.

Red and green make up half of the pie chart.

Warm-Up 187

Check to make sure the student made an appropriate graph.

Answers will vary.

Warm-Up 188

Phil's range was 3. His median was 93. His mode was 93.

Warm-Up 189

The chances of both coins landing on heads is 1 out of 4 or 25%.

Warm-Up 190

The chances of all 3 coins landing on tails is 1 out of 8 or 12.5%.

Warm-Up 191

Barbara rolled 4 odd totals and 6 even totals. She thought she would have a 50-50 chance of getting an odd or even total. Her prediction was correct because 6 out of 10 is 60%, which is close to 50%.

Warm-Up 192

Matt rolled 6 even totals and 4 odd totals. He predicted he would have more odd totals. His prediction was not correct.

Warm-Up 193

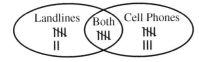

Warm-Up 194

Check to make sure the student made a line graph.

The range is 5. The mode is 5.

Warm-Up 195

A dog is most likely the next patient. Most of the patients that day have been dogs.

Warm-Up 196

The range is 61. The mode is 62. The median is 33.

Warm-Up 197

The chances of having a pop quiz on Monday is 1 out of 5 or a 20% chance. The chances of having a pop quiz on Friday is 5 out of 5 or a 100% chance.

Warm-Up 198

The chances of Selena being picked on the first day is 1 out of 20 or a 5% chance. The chances of Selena being picked on the 15th day is 1 out of 5 or a 20% chance.

Warm-Up 199

Anthony has a 5 out of 9 chance of rolling an odd number and a 4 out of 9 chance of rolling an even number.

Warm-Up 200

Carolyn has a 6 out of 12, or 50%, chance of rolling a number greater than 6 and a 3 out of 12, or 25%, chance of rolling an even number greater than 6.

Warm-Up 201

Check to make sure the student made a graph showing Marisa's results. More people are right-handed than left-handed.

Warm-Up 202

Check to make sure the student made a graph showing Tamika's results. It's not likely to be sunny because for most of the month, it was either raining or snowing.

Warm-Up 203

Marisol has a 100% chance of having recess because recess happens on every school day.

Warm-Up 204

It is not likely that Nigel will be allowed to stay up late on a school night.

Warm-Up 205

Sample questions:

Which hat did more people wear?

Did more people wear cowboy hats or baseball caps?

Warm-Up 206

A line graph would best show Laurel's change in height over the years. Her growth would be easy to see with this kind of graph.

Warm-Up 207

Check to make sure the student chose a graph and explained why he or she chose that graph.

Warm-Up 208

Check to make sure the student made a graph and explained why he or she chose that graph.

Warm-Up 209

It is not likely that Gene will catch a fish as he has never caught a fish before.

Warm-Up 210

It is likely that Thelma will go to the library as she goes either there or to an art class each Saturday.

Warm-Up 211

The numbers are increasing by 6. On the tenth pull, 61 marshmallows will plop out.

Warm-Up 212

The number is doubling each week. On week 5, Phillip will see 64 turtles.

Warm-Up 213

8	3	9	6	4	7	2	1	5
2	7	5	1	3	8	6	4	9
4	6	1	5	2	9	7	8	3
1	9	2	4	7	5	8	3	6
6	5	8	2	1	3	9	7	4
3	4	7	9	8	6	5	2	1
5	1	3	7	6	2	4	9	8
9	2	4	8	5	1	3	6	7
7	8	6	3	9	4	1	5	2

Warm-Up 214

Sample answer:

13	11	18
12	16	14
17	15	10

Warm-Up 215

In all, Mom and Dad earned 994,888 frequent flyer miles.

Warm-Up 216

Grandma has traveled 631,845 more miles.

Warm-Up 217

Osbaldo is 5 years old, Fernando is 7 years old, Shakira is 10 years old, and Maria is 12 years old.

Warm-Up 218

The zebra weighs 900 pounds. The giraffe weighs 1,800 pounds. The tortoise weighs 450 pounds.

Warm-Up 219

Stewart ran 8 laps, and Sonya ran 16 laps.

Warm-Up 220

Maurice sold 24 sports magazines, 12 fashion magazines, and 12 news magazines.

Warm-Up 221

The least amount of money is $2.03: 3 pennies, 3 nickels, 1 dime, 1 quarter, 1 half-dollar, and 1 dollar.

The greatest amount of money is $4.91: 1 penny, 1 nickel, 1 dime, 1 quarter, 3 half-dollars, and 3 dollars.

Warm-Up 222

Jonah has 3 figurines, 2 four-legged animals, and 2 balls in his pocket. Or he has 1 figurine, 3 four-legged animals, and 3 balls.

Warm-Up 223

4 possible arrangements:

Ryan, Candy, Elise, and Jacob

Ryan, Elise, Candy, and Jacob

Jacob, Candy, Elise, and Ryan

Jacob, Elise, Candy, and Ryan

Warm-Up 224

Karina collected 400 pennies, Brandi collected 200 pennies, and Bill collected 100 pennies.

Warm-Up 225

The last number is 121. The rule is to multiply the last number by 3 and add 1.

Warm-Up 226

The last number is 16. The rule is to subtract each number by 8.

Warm-Up 227

$2 \times (4 + 6) = 20$

Warm-Up 228

$6 \times (2 + 4) = 36$

Warm-Up 229

The missing numbers are 21, 27, and 33. The rule is to multiply the "In" number by 3.

Warm-Up 230

The next 3 numbers are 80, 30, and 70. The rule is to subtract 90, add 80, subtract 70, add 60, subtract 50, and add 40. (Reduce the number by 10 each time, alternating addition and subtraction.)

Warm-Up 231

$18 + 13 = 31$ or $13 + 18 = 31$

Warm-Up 232

$41 - 28 = 13$ or $41 - 13 = 28$

Warm-Up 233

Sample answer:

Library book (2 pounds), Math book (3 pounds), Reading book (4 pounds)

Warm-Up 234

Sample answer:

Taylor put 6 blocks in 1 stack, 8 blocks in another stack, and 9 blocks in the final stack.

Warm-Up 235

$27 - x = 19$

$x = 8$

Warm-Up 236

$500 - x = 217$ or $500 - 217 = x$

$x = 283$

Warm-Up 237

The prime numbers are 5, 7, 11, 13, 17, and 19.

Warm-Up 238

No, 51 is not a prime number because $3 \times 17 = 51$.

Warm-Up 239

Divide both sides by 4.

$x = 4$

Warm-Up 240

$x = 5$

Warm-Up 241

$9 \times x = 63$ or $63 \div 9 = x$

$x = 7$

Warm-Up 242

$78 \div x = 3$ or $78 \div 3 = x$

$x = 26$

Warm-Up 243

$2x + x = 12$

$3x = 12$

$x = 4$

Mom bought 8 cans of peaches and 4 cans of pears.

Warm-Up 244

$3x + x = 20$

$4x = 20$

$x = 5$

Dad has 15 nickels and 5 pennies.

Warm-Up 245

The next 3 numbers should be 256; 1,024; and 4,096. The rule is to multiply each number by 4.

Warm-Up 246

The next three numbers will be 1,500; 750; and 375. The rule is to divide each number by 2.

Warm-Up 247

$(23 + 23) + 11 = 57$

Warm-Up 248

$4 \times (10 \times 10) = 400$

Warm-Up 249

$6x = 12$

$x = 2$

Warm-Up 250

$9x = 27$

$x = 3$